A Sultan in Autumn

A Sultan in Autumn
Erdogan Faces Turkey's Uncontainable Forces

Soner Cagaptay

I.B.TAURIS
LONDON • NEW YORK • OXFORD • NEW DELHI • SYDNEY

THE
WASHINGTON INSTITUTE
for Near East Policy

I.B. TAURIS
Bloomsbury Publishing Plc
50 Bedford Square, London, WC1B 3DP, UK
1385 Broadway, New York, NY 10018, USA
29 Earlsfort Terrace, Dublin 2, Ireland

BLOOMSBURY, I.B. TAURIS and the I.B. Tauris logo are trademarks of
Bloomsbury Publishing Plc

First published in Great Britain 2022

A catalogue record for this book is available from the British Library.

Library of Congress Cataloging-in-Publication Data
Names: Çağaptay, Soner, author.
Title: A sultan in autumn: Erdogan faces Turkey's uncontainable forces /
Soner Cagaptay.
Description: New York : I.B. Tauris, 2021.
Includes bibliographical references and index.
Identifiers: LCCN 2021028261 (print) | LCCN 2021028262 (ebook) |
ISBN 9780755642809 (paperback) | ISBN 9780755642793 (hardback) |
ISBN 9780755642816 (epub) | ISBN 9780755642823 (pdf) |
ISBN 9780755642830 (ebook other)
Subjects: LCSH: Erdoğan, Recep Tayyip. | Turkey--Politics and government--1980-
Classification: LCC DR605.E73 C33 2021 (print) | LCC DR605.E73 (ebook) |
DDC 320.5409561--dc23
LC record available at https://lccn.loc.gov/2021028261
LC ebook record available at https://lccn.loc.gov/2021028262g

ISBN: HB: 9780755642793
PB: 9780755642809
ePDF: 9780755642816
ePub: 9780755642823

Printed and bound in Great Britain

To find out more about our authors and books visit www.bloomsbury.com and
sign up for our newsletters

To the future of democratic societies
in Turkey and around the world.

Contents

Acknowledgments

I would like to thank my research assistants Deniz Yuksel and Reilly Barry and research intern Ilke Arkan for editing various drafts of this book, as well as helping with research and the endnotes. Ilke and fellow research intern Ayse Nur Dil Barutcu also assisted with fact-checking. Reilly helped during all phases of writing and editing, and I owe her a tremendous debt of gratitude since I could not have finished this book without her. I also owe big thanks to many friends for reviewing various drafts. Finally, I would like to thank editor Jason Warshof and designer Maria Radacsi for their work on this book. Jason's editing helped improve the manuscript significantly, and I am grateful to him for that. All omissions and errors are, of course, mine.

Washington DC
April 1, 2021

Abbreviations

AKP	Justice and Development Party
CHP	Republican People's Party
DEVA	Democracy and Progress Party
Diyanet	Directorate of Religious Affairs
FP, or Fazilet	Virtue Party
Gelecek	Future Party
GNA	Government of National Accord (Libya)
HDP	Peoples' Democratic Party
IS	Islamic State
IYI	Good Party
MHP	Nationalist Action Party
MSP	National Salvation Party
LNA	Libyan National Army
PKK	Kurdistan Workers Party
RP, or Refah	Welfare Party
SP, or Saadet	Felicity Party
TRT	Turkish Radio and Television
YPG	People's Defense Units (Syria)

Preface

I was born and raised in Turkey and have studied Turkish politics for more than two decades. Since 1996, I have lived in the United States. Here and overseas, I frequently give lectures addressing audiences ranging from diplomats to citizens interested in global affairs. I also provide commentary for print media and networks, from the BBC to the *New York Times*.

In 2017, I wrote the first-ever English-language biography of Turkish president Recep Tayyip Erdogan, *The New Sultan: Erdogan and the Crisis of Modern Turkey*.[1] Unsurprisingly, I am therefore often asked in public appearances questions such as what kind of leader Erdogan is and what drives his policies. Lately, I am also asked how the rising opposition and the Turkish economy, which entered recession in 2018 and then slumped in 2020 amid the Covid-19 pandemic, will shape Erdogan's future policies.[2]

A good metaphor for Turkey is that of the onion, and this is one reason I enjoy studying it. Analytically speaking, the country is all layers but has virtually no "core." Just as you think you have grasped Turkey's "essence," a new layer emerges, forcing you to reconsider everything you previously thought you knew. Turkey defies simplistic generalizations and Manichean dualisms alike. Is Erdogan an autocratic leader? Yes. But will Turkey's democracy and populace wither under him? No. Turkey's democracy is resilient, its civil society robust, and its cohort of younger voters increasingly unhappy with the president's style of governance.

Imagine the proverbial act of hammering a square peg into a round hole, and you can conceive of Erdogan's conundrum—his challenge in trying to keep control of the forces that constitute today's Turkey. Since Turkey became a multiparty democracy in 1950, none of its leaders—from Adnan Menderes in the 1950s to Turgut Ozal in the 1980s—has succeeded in sustaining one-person rule in the country, regardless of their popularity.

Despite his lengthy tenure, I do not think Erdogan will break this trend. A country of 84 million citizens with an economy worth over $1 trillion in 2020 (measured according to current prices), along with a highly active civil society, large middle class, and tradition of robust democratic traditions, is too complex and diverse demographically, too large economically, and too complicated politically to simply become the province of one individual leader.

Like Turkey itself, Erdogan is a fascinating figure who often defies black-and-white characterizations. He controls Turkey, but as I explain below, he no longer truly leads it. He was born and raised in a poor Istanbul neighborhood but today lives in a palace with more than a thousand rooms in the Turkish capital, Ankara, as the country's quasi-sultan. He fights against the elites for the interests of the common voter but himself embodies state, military, and religious power in Turkey. Last but not least, he is neither a dictator nor a democrat.

But one aspect of Erdogan's career can be cast in black and white. He is among the inventors of nativist populist politics globally in the twenty-first century. Not unlike other nativist populist leaders, including former U.S. president Donald Trump, Erdogan has a base that loves him, but also—and inversely—an opposition that simply loathes him and is eager to prosecute him should he fall from power.

And herein lies his key challenge: although Erdogan's popularity is waning, he cannot afford to be voted out in elections. Erdogan is only about Erdogan. From now on, he will try to cover all his bases—simultaneously—to increase his chances for political survival. Every step he takes at home—unveiling a new "democratic reform package" in 2021 to restore his image in Washington and with global markets, even as he oppresses his opposition more harshly and creates deeper societal polarization—is meant to safeguard his career. The same can be said about his foreign policy bid to play Russian president Vladimir Putin and U.S. president Joe Biden—again simultaneously.

Specifically, Erdogan's twin goals are to boost the Turkish economy and his base. To this end, he will try to cherry-pick his way to success at the ballot box, again covering all his bases: demonizing the Kurdish nationalist opposition to rally his nationalist base, while legislating more de facto freedoms to appeal to markets; cracking down on vulnerable groups such as the LGBT community and women to appeal to conservative voters, while attempting to revive ties with the European Union and befriending President Biden.

With Biden in the White House, I am now also often asked by journalists about prospects for U.S.-Turkish relations in the Biden-Erdogan era. Enter—once again—Erdogan's survival instincts, specifically his evolving relationship with Russian president Putin. Erdogan made a Faustian bargain with Russia's president (explained in chapter 6) in August 2016 when the latter invited him to Saint Petersburg, following the failed Turkish coup attempt the previous month. During that visit, Putin offered Erdogan support and a power-sharing opportunity in Syria, while likely seeking, in return, Erdogan's commitment to purchase the Russian-made S-400 missile-defense system, hence creating a permanent wedge in U.S.-Turkish ties.

Since that meeting, U.S.-Turkish relations have indeed deteriorated. What is more, the Erdogan-Putin relationship has developed new power-sharing branches, however tenuous they may be, stretching from Syria to the wars in Libya and the South Caucasus, where Ankara and Moscow back opposing sides. In other words, Erdogan is now too deeply enmeshed in his relationship with Putin, and Ankara is exposed to Moscow's vicissitudes in key conflict areas both near and surrounding Turkey. Further—in part because he knows Ankara's purchase of the S-400 system will undermine U.S.-Turkish ties—Putin will not allow Erdogan to renege on the deal. The latter understands he must play along or else face Putin's wrath in Syria, Libya, and the South Caucasus. Putin can easily puncture Erdogan's global strongman image, which the Turkish leader relies on domestically to boost his base. A further risk exists in the more than two million Syrian refugees who could arrive in Turkey should Putin greenlight an Assad regime assault on Idlib, the last rebel-held province in Syria. With anti-refugee sentiment rising in Turkey, even Erdogan would be unable to manage the economic burdens and political trends triggered by such a development.

Making matters worse on the foreign policy front, the United States has already sanctioned Ankara for its purchase of the S-400 system.[3] On December 14, 2020, President Trump imposed some of these sanctions officially on the Presidency of Defense Industries in Turkey before leaving office; this was also a response to Turkish testing of the system two months earlier.[4] This means any major improvement in U.S.-Turkish ties will remain shadowed by the S-400 issue—and perhaps undermined by further U.S. sanctions against Ankara—should Putin use his many levers, including the threat of tourism and trade sanctions targeting Turkey's weak economy, to force Erdogan to retest or even activate the system. In other words, in the next three years, Erdogan will play with both Biden and Putin, but he will ultimately be forced to pick Putin.

Nevertheless, Erdogan's survival instinct will inevitably coax him to attempt to charm Biden. Erdogan will try—desperately—to reach out to and build ties with Biden in 2021 because he sorely needs to calm markets' fears over Turkey's autocratic trajectory. He believes photo ops with Biden are the right message for markets, convincing investors that Turkey is again safe for investment. While many issues continue to divide Ankara and Washington, from the S-400 deal to continued U.S. cooperation with Syria-based People's Defense Units (YPG), a Kurdish group linked to the Turkey-based Kurdistan Workers Party (PKK)—which is designated as a terrorist organization by Turkey, the United States, and other NATO members—Erdogan will try to brush this all aside in the short term. In fact, as of early 2021 the Turkish leader, for the first time in many years, believes he needs Washington more than Washington needs him. Erdogan is convinced he must create a narrative of good ties with the United States (and Europe) in order to restore strong economic growth in Turkey.

Erdogan's motive here: once again, survival. Due to periods of recession and slowing economic growth since 2018—and beginning with the 2019 Turkish local elections—the president has lost his former popular majority. The next parliamentary and presidential elections in Turkey, scheduled for 2023, could well deliver a surprise.

If voters were to humble Erdogan again as they did in 2019, picking opposition candidates, notwithstanding his control of the country's media and influence over the electoral boards, he might simply refuse to accept the outcome, claiming falsely, for instance, that the polls were rigged—i.e., "pulling a Trump." Given Biden's own experience with Trump's defiance in the United States in 2020–21, the latter will have scant sympathy for Erdogan under such a scenario.

Similarly, Biden will find it hard to embrace Erdogan if and when the latter arrests more opposition leaders, and further tramples democratic checks and balances to stack odds in his favor in Turkey's next elections. In other words, in the next three years, Biden will be forced to pick between democracy and Erdogan, and he will pick democracy.

In writing this short book during the pandemic lockdown of 2020, I wanted to explain Erdogan's leadership style, often Janus-faced politics, calculations, and survival instincts, particularly over his nearly two decades in national power. The broader goal was to put his current and upcoming challenges—first at home, then in foreign policy, including ties with the United States—in context. I have also sought to offer an educated prediction of what is to come for the leader, for Turkey, and for the rest of the world in relation to Turkey.

Notes

1 Soner Cagaptay, *The New Sultan: Erdogan and the Crisis of Modern Turkey* (London: I.B. Tauris, 2017).

2 Ezgi Erkoyun, "Turkish Economy to Shrink for First Time in a Decade This Year: Reuters Poll," Reuters, April 21, 2020, https://www.reuters.com/article/us-turkey-economy-poll/turkish-economy-to-shrink-for-first-time-in-a-decade-this-year-reuters-poll-idUSKCN2231GV.

3 William Mauldin, "U.S. Sanctions Turkish Entities over Acquisition of Russian Defense System," *Wall Street Journal*, December 14, 2020, https://www.wsj.com/articles/u-s-sanctions-turkish-entities-over-acquisition-of-russian-defense-system-11607970686.

4 Amanda Macias, "U.S. Sanctions Turkey over Purchase of Russian S-400 Missile System," CNBC, December 14, 2020, https://www.cnbc.com/2020/12/14/us-sanctions-turkey-over-russian-s400.html.

Introduction

Recep Tayyip Erdogan is a consequential leader in the context of Turkish history. He has won more than a dozen nationwide elections since 2002, primarily by delivering strong economic growth, increasing access to the proverbial pie, and improving social services. His popularity has, in turn, allowed him to eliminate key elements of Turkey's twentieth-century political system, labeled Kemalism, while also casting Turkey as a prickly member of the international order, quarreling with and often pushing back against allies, from the United States to France to Germany, as well as neighbors, from Greece to Iran to Syria.

For over half a century, Kemalism prohibited religion in government officially, as well as subordinating religion institutionally, but Erdogan, especially since around 2010, has flooded Turkey's government, education system, and public sphere with his version of conservative Islam. This has swelled the ranks of his Kemalist enemies. Many secular, liberal, and leftist Turkish citizens, including Kurdish nationalists, loathe Erdogan equally. As a nativist populist leader, Erdogan demonizes, brutalizes, and cracks down on these demographic groups, which he believes will not vote for him in any case. Many of Erdogan's opponents are, therefore, eager to see him lose the country's next general elections, currently scheduled for 2023, so that they can prosecute him through the court system and target him more generally for his misdeeds, all with the goal of diminishing his stature and legacy.

In the foreign policy realm, Erdogan's interventionist and nationalist policies have alienated many among Turkey's European allies, most recently France. Among other areas of tension, Paris and Ankara have engaged in a proxy war in Libya, supporting opposing sides in that country's civil war (as explained in chapter 7). His policies, specifically support to the Muslim Brotherhood during the Arab uprisings that began in 2011, have undermined Turkey's ties to Israel, Egypt, and Gulf Cooperation Council members such as Saudi Arabia and the United Arab Emirates, countries that see the Brotherhood as the greatest threat to their security.

Iran, too, opposes Turkey's policies in the Middle East, most notably Ankara's support for the anti-Assad rebels in Syria. For a time, this support put Turkey on a collision course with Assad's other international patron—and Turkey's historical nemesis—Russia. While Erdogan has recently made peace with Putin, Moscow can hardly be considered a friend to Ankara in the strategic sense. Turkey and Russia disagree on a plethora of issues, ranging from Russia's 2014 annexation of Crimea to the older Cyprus conflict.

To be fair to Erdogan, not everything looks bleak from Ankara. The Turkish president has managed to maintain good ties with a number of states, including Qatar, Azerbaijan, Ukraine, and Britain.

However, owing to sharp policy differences over Syria and the Arab uprisings explained in this book, Turkey's ties with its oldest and most important ally, the United States, have weakened considerably under Erdogan. Simply put, Erdogan cannot rely on Turkey's seven-decade-long ally to reliably cover for Ankara. This presents difficulties: Erdogan must constantly manage his relationship with Putin in Syria, Libya, and the South Caucasus, where Ankara and Moscow support opposing sides in conflicts. Erdogan's game plan: continue to play everyone, including Russia, but also the United States, European countries, Iran, and Arab states, against one another.

The economy is Erdogan's Achilles' heel, both at home and in foreign policy, where it will determine whether he can continue his juggling act with international players. After enjoying some fifteen years of growth, Turkey's economy entered recession in 2018, which may be why his faction lost mayoral elections in Istanbul, Ankara, and other key Turkish cities the following year, and with that his popular majority. In addition, when Erdogan nullified the Istanbul outcome on March 29, 2019, which his party lost by a narrow 13,000 votes, the opposition delivered him a resounding beating in the revote—the first such electoral reversal for him. His candidate, Binali Yildirim, lost by nearly a million votes.

There was a time when Erdogan—whether one liked him or not—represented change in Turkey. He stood for a forward-looking vision for the country, and there was hope that he could navigate the most pressing challenges, from the Kurdish issue to corruption to economic mismanagement, and he did. For instance, after taking office as prime minister in 2003, he delivered a decade of economic growth, a record achievement in recent Turkish history. And in 2011, he entered into secret peace talks with the Kurdistan Workers Party (PKK) to find a political solution to Turkey's Kurdish problem. The people loved him for his effectiveness and supported him at the ballot box. But today, Erdogan appears to have lost his magic touch. He no longer represents change in Turkey. Now, he stands for the status quo, including problems locked in by his own errors (e.g., ineffective monetary policy, the S-400 deal, and personal acrimony with regional leaders). And the opposition, which has proven resilient, represents change and problem-solving. To put it succinctly, although Erdogan controls Turkey, he does not lead it anymore.

Today Erdogan is, therefore, a leader in trouble. And unfortunately, many of the ways he fights to retain power actually facilitate the greatest threats to Turkey's strength. For instance, to divert attention from the economy, governance issues, and rising opposition at home, he has since 2018 been aggressively seeking conflicts into which to interject Turkey. To be fair, Erdogan is not *creating* these conflicts. In a world where the United States is retreating from global commitments and interventions, Turkey's neighborhood is rife with wars. Erdogan knows well enough, however, to align foreign policy distractions with

Turkey's real foreign policy concerns, from the eastern Mediterranean to the South Caucasus.

As of early 2021, this strategy has resulted in Turkish military involvement in wars in Syria, Libya, and the South Caucasus, as well as mutually driven crises between Ankara and fellow NATO members France and Greece. Rallying public opinion around war and national security issues seems to have prevented further erosion of Erdogan's popularity in the short term. The military interventions may have even brought short-term gains. But at what ultimate cost?

If the hobbled Turkish economy fails to grow strongly, not only will Erdogan's base keep weakening, but he will be unable to continue with his foreign policy game. The odds could thus steepen against Erdogan generally.

But one of the things that makes Erdogan such an intriguing figure to study is his ability to beat the odds. Can he survive the Covid pandemic, the economic crisis, a resilient opposition, demographic challenges, and multiple wars? In this book, I make the case for his probable survival, but one with unfortunate costs for Turkey's citizens, institutions, and allies. I also describe why and how I think he will manage his various challenges, and what effect his continued leadership will have on Turkey's future, as well as ties between Ankara and its friends and neighbors.

The Underdog

Since he first entered national politics in the 1990s as mayor of Istanbul, Erdogan cast himself as a poor man from the other side of the tracks. Similar to Turkey's own past populist leaders such as Suleyman Demirel and Bulent Ecevit, Erdogan has always rooted his political identity in standing up for common people, advocating for their interests against the elites. But to understand Erdogan's politics, one must first understand his upbringing and early political career in a country then dominated by the secularist ideology of its founder, Mustafa Kemal Ataturk.

Erdogan was born in 1954 to a poor, pious, and socially conservative family in Istanbul's gritty, working-class Kasimpasa neighborhood.[1] His parents had migrated to Istanbul from a conservative province in the country's Black Sea hinterland; his father's personality was what one might call extremely authoritarian. Erdogan felt profoundly marginalized growing up poor and religious in the old Turkey, where any public role for religion was banned.

A Pamuk Character

In his novel *A Strangeness in My Mind*, the Turkish Nobel laureate Orhan Pamuk portrays Mevlut, a poor, conservative immigrant from

Anatolia—the Asian part of Turkey—who grew up in Istanbul in the 1960s and 1970s only to come to hate the city's secular, Westernized elites.[2] Recep Tayyip Erdogan might be conceived as a slightly earlier version of Mevlut. When Erdogan grew up in Kasimpasa in the 1950s and 1960s, Turkey was a poor and underdeveloped country.

Located in the heart of the city, Kasimpasa sits at the bottom of a hill that ascends to Istanbul's bohemian Beyoglu district, and then to Nisantasi, the city's exclusive upper-crust, old-money enclave. During Erdogan's childhood, Nisantasi was a refuge for the privileged few who would sip cocktails in high-end hotels and shop for expensive clothing on nearby leafy boulevards. The sights and sounds of Kasimpasa, situated along the Golden Horn—the famed, narrow waterway that cleaves the European side of Istanbul—could not have been more different from Nisantasi.

Understanding Erdogan requires dissecting his upbringing in twentieth-century secularist Turkey as a pious man, his mistreatment by the country's elites, and his subsequent rise to power in 2003 as part of an ascendant movement: political Islam.

…Meets Political Islam

Erdogan cut his political teeth in the 1970s in Turkey's National Salvation Party (MSP), and its National Outlook school, a deeply nationalist, anti-Semitic and anti-Western, conservative, and avowedly anti-secular movement. By the 1990s, he had risen through the hierarchy of the Welfare Party (RP), the MSP's successor, and in 2001 he founded his own bloc, the Justice and Development Party (AKP), with help from fellow RP member Abdullah Gul.

The AKP emerged from Erdogan's own dual heritage: as a son of Turkey's greatest city and commercial capital—and thus a man who is pragmatic, business-minded, and eager for global recognition—and simultaneously as a political Islamist deeply hostile to the secular elites who dominated Istanbul throughout the twentieth century, while also never fully able to embrace Europe or the United States. Erdogan effectively conquered the historical Ottoman capital, serving a successful stint as mayor between 1994 and 1998, before setting his sights on the whole of Turkey. In 2002, Erdogan's AKP entered the Turkish parliament as the country's largest party.

Nevertheless, Erdogan's rise to power was never smooth, with guardians of the secularist system seeking to block and punish him at every step. In 1998, for example, he was forced to step down as Istanbul's mayor and sent to jail for reciting a poem ruled by judges to be incendiary. Speaking to a crowd in the southeastern Turkish province of Siirt, Erdogan delivered the following verses: "The mosques are our barracks, the domes our helmets, the minarets our bayonets, and the faithful our soldiers..."[3] His original ten-month sentence was eventually reduced to just over four months, but his imprisonment, from March to July 1999, was accompanied by his disbarment from Turkish politics. This temporary injury, however, ended up empowering Erdogan by casting him as a martyr, in turn boosting his appeal among conservative constituencies and poorer voters. Thus, ironically, secularist attempts to undermine Erdogan, in the end, helped him.

The AKP thrived on the "underdog" label in the November 2002 parliamentary election. But even then, Erdogan faced hurdles associated with the secularist system. According to the Turkish constitution at the time, the prime minister also served as a member of parliament, but Erdogan's political ban prevented him from running for the legislature, and thus from taking office as prime minister. Only in February 2003, when he was allowed to run in a special election for Siirt province, was he able to enter parliament. Erdogan finally took office as Turkey's prime minister on March 14, 2003.

Notes

1   Soner Cagaptay, *The New Sultan: Erdogan and the Crisis of Modern Turkey* (London: I.B. Tauris, 2017).

2   Orhan Pamuk, *A Strangeness in My Mind* (New York: Knopf Doubleday, 2015).

3   "Turkey's Charismatic Pro-Islamic Leader," *The New York Times*, November 4, 2002.

Erdogan's Turkey at a Glance

Recep Tayyip Erdogan's national political career can be broken down into three periods: 2003–10, an era of bright economic growth, which he used to boost his popularity but also to undermine democratic checks and balances and consolidate power; 2011–18, an era of political polarization, during which he demonized and brutalized his opposition to strengthen his base; and 2018–present, during which Erdogan has dropped even the pretense of democratic norms in order to prevent Turkey's opposition forces from surging and overpowering him.

At this moment, the challenge for Erdogan is to neutralize the rising political forces that oppose him.[1] Some related dynamics, such as younger citizens' mounting resentment of him, his government's inability to meet heightened economic expectations, and rising, vigilant opposition, are of his own creation. Other obstacles are not, at least not directly—for instance, potential refugee flows from Syria that would not only increase by more than 50 percent Turkey's existing Syrian refugee population (now at nearly four million) but also trigger anti-refugee, anti-Erdogan political movements that even he might struggle to control.

In short, because of factors both within and outside his control, Erdogan's nearly two-decade grip on national power could be loosening. But how he reacts to this crisis entails many uncertainties.

Erdogan is among the inventors of nativist populist politics in the twenty-first century. He knows how to polarize the electorate to boost his base. He knows how to oppress his opposition to secure election victories. And he is likely to cling to power by hook or by crook, albeit without his long-accustomed aura of omnipotence.

For those thinking Turkish politics looked unstable and Erdogan authoritarian recently, the ride will only get bumpier as the president faces stiffer challenges. Moreover, Turkey is the oldest democracy and largest economy between Germany and India; Erdogan's moves will therefore have ramifications beyond Turkey's borders.

Together with his nativist politics, Erdogan offers a legitimate record, until recently, of delivering economic growth, helping him amass a base of mostly right-wing supporters. While the 2019 municipal election in Istanbul showed these voters have started to abandon the Turkish president, mainly because he was no longer delivering the same levels of prosperity,[2] others seem to resent his growing control of institutions at the heart of longstanding and widely embraced democratic traditions in Turkey.

Since 2002, Erdogan and his AKP have won elections mainly on a platform of strong economic growth. His base loves him not only because he has lifted many voters out of poverty, but also because he has improved living standards nationwide. For instance, Turkish citizens saw near record low unemployment near 9 percent in 2013.[3] Inflation, in the high double digits and often triple digits for decades, fell into the single digits under Erdogan. This along with a new mortgage system allowed many Turkish citizens to buy their first homes and to acquire wealth. Also, according to a 2013 study, the "neonatal mortality rate in Turkey has declined within 8 years similar to that reached by Organization for Economic Co-operation and Development countries over 30 years."[4]

By mid-2019, however, unemployment had jumped to nearly 14 percent, even as the economy had technically exited its brief recession.[5]

With a weakened lira, surging external debt, and low foreign currency reserves, the Turkish economy was already fragile before the onset of the pandemic in early 2020. Turkey could face more economic troubles, further testing Erdogan.

In fact, he has already faced a setback partly caused by economics: his party's defeat in the 2019 mayoral elections in Istanbul, Ankara, and other key cities—dealing a blow to his political brand. In March 2019, Erdogan annulled the results of the Istanbul vote on the grounds of "irregularities"[6] considered unconvincing by independent observers.[7] His party had lost by a narrow 13,000 votes. Perhaps he had thought his control of national media and institutions, including the electoral commission itself, would guarantee a victory the second time around, but it did not. His faction, led by candidate Binali Yildirim, lost the second round, held June 23, 2019, by 800,000 votes. The outcome—more than sixty times the original margin—reflects the demise of Erdogan's popularity especially among young voters. The do-over also appeared to demonstrate the resilience of Turkey's democratic opposition and traditions. Turkey is bigger than Erdogan—a democracy with a history of free and fair elections stretching back to 1950—and Erdogan will have a difficult time completely subjugating the country to his will.

The resulting troubles for Erdogan are also worrisome for Turkey—because of the president's dark impulses. Over the years, Erdogan has brutalized many constituencies; protestors have been beaten and killed in the past decade specifically. Since the failed coup attempt in 2016, his government has imprisoned an estimated 50,000 people as detainees. More than 150,000 academics and journalists and others were removed from their jobs on suspicion of political opposition in the aftermath of the failed putsch. Following the coup, Erdogan used the state of emergency powers given to him to go after not only coup plotters but the broader opposition too. To put it simply, citizens, many not linked to the coup attempt, have been punished merely for criticizing or opposing Erdogan. And during a 2016 visit to Washington, his bodyguards pummeled American protestors on a public lawn, on camera, for the world to see.[8] The groups that Erdogan has targeted inside Turkey, mostly composed of leftists or liberals, simply hate him. Another, more conservative group—former AKP members, including former finance minister Ali Babacan and prime minister Ahmet Davutoglu, who have defected as they grow increasingly disillusioned with Erdogan's abandonment of their neoliberal pact—also stands poised to challenge his control of the center-right. In short, if Erdogan loses power, trouble likely awaits him. His fears of legal prosecution by the groups he has targeted and demonized over the years, should they seize power, are not unfounded.

Prepandemic polls already showed Erdogan's popularity flagging, and a May 2020 survey showed opposition politicians, such as Ankara mayor Mansur Yavas, having a stronger public rating for "managing the pandemic" than does Erdogan.[9] Meral Aksener, who leads a smaller nationalist and center-right faction, the Good Party (IYI), was closely trailing Erdogan in public confidence, suggesting that even some of the nationalists in his voter base might be peeling away.[10]

Erdogan must sense that he will emerge from the pandemic with weaker public support. Until recently, he has run Turkey with a strong plurality, and at times a near majority, but from now on he will have to rely on nationalist minority support to maintain his rule. Realizing this, Erdogan will surely try to poach support elsewhere for his AKP, as he has done with the Nationalist Action Party (MHP) since 2017. Luckily for Erdogan, Turkey's next parliamentary and presidential elections are not scheduled until 2023.

Younger voters further complicate the president's future. Those between the ages of eighteen and forty make up around a quarter of the country's population, and voters and future voters between fifteen and thirty will total nearly 20 million by 2023. In the view of this constituency, Erdogan has sole ownership of Turkey and all its problems.[11] What is more, these citizens who have grown up under Erdogan's socially conservative and increasingly autocratic rule, among all Turkey's demographic cohorts, seem least inclined to embrace his top-down, religiously conservative agenda.

Economic, demographic, and political trends may be working against Erdogan, but if precedent holds, he will do whatever it takes to remain Turkey's president. He will do all he can to prevent his opposition from voting him out, even though numbers will work against him at the polls, which means increased oppression before, during, and after the elections. Barring a surprise peaceful transfer of power, he will likely unleash significantly sharper waves of political and ideological repression to maintain control.

Practically, in seeking to maintain power, Erdogan's next challenge will be to contain the seemingly uncontainable forces arrayed against him, mostly rooted in the country's domestic opposition but also among the AKP's old guard. In response, an era of intensified authoritarianism and nativist populism, already pervasive in the country, will emerge that is unprecedented even in the context of the recent Erdogan years.

Like Turkey itself, Erdogan's politics also—often—defies black-and-white generalizations. Thus, the Turkish leader will likely unveil a "democratic reform package" in 2021, promising to improve the rule of law and democracy to restore Turkey's image in Washington and for international markets. Erdogan's complicated double game will be to create a semblance of democratic relaxation at home in order to build ties with President Biden and attract investment to Turkey, while at the same time actually dividing and oppressing his opposition and continuing to polarize the Turkish population.

Understanding how Erdogan consolidated his grip on Turkish politics sheds light on his status as Turkey's "eternal president." An analysis of the Erdogan reign and strategies—the themes of this book—can provide an illuminating glimpse of his future and Turkey's.

Notes

1   E. Fuat Keyman and Andrew O'Donohue, "The Five Challenges to Erdogan's Executive Presidential Rule After the Coronavirus," German Marshall Fund of the United States, September 9, 2020, https://www. gmfus.org/publications/five-challenges-erdogans-executive-presidential-rule-after-coronavirus.

2   Orhan Coskun and Can Sezer, "Erdogan on Track to Lose Turkey's Biggest Cities in Shock Poll Upset," BBC, March 31, 2019, https://www. reuters.com/article/us-turkey-election/erdogan-on-track-to-lose-turkeys-biggest-cities-in-shock-poll-upset-idUSKCN1RD130.

3   "Labor Force Statistics, 2013," Turkiye Istatistik Kurumu, https://data. tuik.gov.tr/Bulten/Index?p=Hanehalki-Isgucu-Istatistikleri-2013-16015.

4   Gamze Demirel, "Rapid Decrease of Neonatal Mortality in Turkey," *Maternal and Child Health Journal*, September 2013, https://pubmed. ncbi.nlm.nih.gov/22945874/.

5   H. Plecher, "Turkey: Unemployment Rate from 1999 to 2019," Statista, July 15, 2020, https://www.statista.com/statistics/263708/ unemployment-rate-in-turkey/. For the 2018 recession, see Sevgi Ceren Gokkoyun, "Issizlik Rakamlari Aciklandi," Anadolu Agency, March 20, 2020, https://www.aa.com.tr/tr/ekonomi/issizlik-rakamlari-aciklandi/1772668.

6   "Election Board to Have Last Say on Poll Results in Istanbul and Ankara," *Hurriyet Daily News*, April 2, 2019, https://www. hurriyetdailynews.com/election-board-to-have-last-say-on-poll-results-in-istanbul-and-ankara-142380.

7   "Piero Fassino (SOC): 'An Undemocratic Decision in Istanbul,'" Council of Europe, May 9, 2019, https://bit.ly/3oLrIRF.

8   "Recep Tayyip Erdogan: Turkey's Pugnacious President," BBC, October 27, 2020, https://www.bbc.com/news/world-europe-13746679.

9   "Anket Aciklandi: Mansur Yavas, Erdogan'i Geride Birakti," *Cumhuriyet*, May 6, 2020.

10 Ozer Sencar (@ozersencar1), "Meral Aksener'in populariteti Kasim 2019'dan bu yana belirgin sekilde artmis. Parti liderleri arasinda

popularitesi en yuksek ikinci olmus. Dikkate deger bir durum," post on Twitter, May 6, 2020, 6:54 a.m., https://twitter.com/ozersencar1/status/1257987136898375681.

11 Max Hoffman, "Turkey's President Erdogan Is Losing Ground at Home," Center for American Progress, August 24, 2020, https://www.americanprogress.org/issues/security/reports/2020/08/24/489727/turkeys-president-erdogan-losing-ground-home/.

3

Conqueror of Kemalism

Turkey's early twentieth-century leaders were known as "Kemalists" after Mustafa Kemal Ataturk—the country's first president and founder of the Turkish republic in 1923. They believed Ataturk's legacy could not be torn down in a thousand years' time. As a revolutionary leader, Ataturk ruled Turkey until his death in 1938. But much of his legacy, including the Europe-facing, assertively secularist political system that relegated religion to the private sphere, survived only a matter of decades, into the twenty-first century.

Ataturk's contemporary followers admiringly labeled him "*ebedi sef*" (eternal chief). But since the founding leader's death more than eight decades ago, Recep Tayyip Erdogan—who served as prime minister in 2003–14 and has been president since then—has emerged as the country's leader of comparable consequence. It took him less than a decade to tear down many key pillars of Ataturk's system, with significant ramifications for Turkish society. In particular, he has made conservative Islam a guiding principle for Turkish politics and jettisoned a Western orientation for "multi-axial diplomacy" by growing roots in the Middle East, Africa, and Eurasia, and catering to populist impulses—combining his nativist agenda with a militaristic foreign policy stance from Syria to Libya—in Muslim-majority countries.

Erdogan is adoringly called *"reis"* (master) and even "eternal master" by his followers, and could well rule Turkey so long as he is alive, notwithstanding the Covid-19 pandemic, economic downturn, rising opposition, or foreign policy challenges. Yet Erdogan faces one key challenge that Ataturk did not—the need for a democratic mandate. Should the edifice collapse, Erdogan, its architect, will see his stature suffer profoundly. But populists like Erdogan do not refrain from bending the democratic system to their will, and past experience suggests the president will do whatever it takes to block his ouster through the ballot.

Spreading the Cloak of Islam

Having governed Turkey for eighteen years, Erdogan has amassed powers sufficient to undermine Ataturk's legacy and make those original Kemalists, were they still living, blush at their absolute confidence in the system. He has dismantled much of Ataturk's French-style secularism, and with little mercy for his opponents. He has flooded the country's political and education systems with an interpretation of rigidly conservative Sunni Islam and pivoted Turkey away from Europe and the West. This relentless pursuit of top-down social engineering is—paradoxically—Erdogan's "Ataturk" side. Of course, Erdogan does not share Ataturk's values, just his methods. Just as Ataturk shaped Turkey in his own image following the collapse of the Ottoman Empire, Erdogan is dramatically reshaping the country, reflecting a profoundly Muslim identity in politics and foreign policy—and seeking to make it a Great Power once again.

Istanbul—Turkey's cultural and commercial capital, although not its administrative one—is a city of mosques and the politics surrounding them. Just as Erdogan is now demonstrating his power by building a cavernous Camlica Mosque in the city, Ataturk had previously done so by converting the Hagia Sophia Mosque into a secular museum in 1935. Hagia Sophia, originally the city's Byzantine-era cathedral church, was turned into a mosque in 1453 by Sultan Mehmed II. Through this representational and political act of "undoing a mosque," Ataturk ssignaled his desire to detach religion from politics.

While Ataturk "de-mosqued" Hagia Sophia to underline his vision, Erdogan's patronage of the grand Camlica Mosque, already dubbed "Erdogan's mosque," testifies to his own vision for his rule and for the former imperial city. The "new Turkey" sought by Erdogan is a profoundly Islamic and socially conservative society, one facing the Middle East and where Islam is enmeshed in politics, instead of firewalled from it. In July 2020, in a religious ceremony, moreover, Erdogan reconsecrated Hagia Sophia as a mosque, underlining his political Islamist refashioning of Turkey.

Erdogan's political Islamism does not mean he cannot, for now, live with Turkey's secularist constitution. The president has been spreading Islamic rules and mores across the country without a big bang and bloody revolution à la Iran 1979.

In the United States and Europe, sharia is often associated with corporal punishment, such as beheadings carried out by Islamist extremists and the likes of the Islamic State. But in fact, only a few countries, such as Iran and Saudi Arabia, enact sharia in this form.

Most Muslim-majority countries have a mix of religious and secular laws, which invite the implementation of other, less draconian forms of sharia. In these instances, sharia feeds into a complex web of legal, political, and administrative measures. Blending with state power, it imposes Islamic practices on the public, such as fasting during Ramadan. Conservative clerics and politicians who claim to interpret or uphold sharia also often demonize nonpracticing members of society and seek to punish speech or acts deemed offensive to Islam.[1]

In its widely seen practice, sharia is therefore not the axe of the executioner, but rather an impermeable veil that envelops society. Many pious Muslims individually choose to abide by some or all tenets of sharia, which guides their religiosity. But, as a political force, sharia draws its power from governmental and societal pressure mechanisms (as explained below). Together, they coerce citizens to adhere to conservative readings of Islam.

In recent years, Turkish officials have broken with decades of precedent in what is still, at least nominally, a secular republic: they have begun describing the country's military deployment in Syria as "jihad."[2] During the first two days of Operation Olive Branch in Syria's Afrin region, which began January 20, 2018, the government's Directorate of Religious Affairs *ordered* all Turkey's nearly 90,000 mosques to broadcast the "al-Fath" chapter from the Quran—"the prayer of conquest"—through the loudspeakers on their minarets.[3] Mainstreaming jihad, which sanctions violence against those who "offend Islam," is a crucial step in casting the veil of sharia over a society.

Turkey had for decades managed to keep sharia out of the official sphere, making it an outlier, together with Tunisia and a few others, among Muslim-majority countries. While the secular constitutional system remains, recent developments in Turkey together demonstrate a shift.

The Erdogan-led government has been limiting individual freedoms, as well as sanctioning individuals who "insult Islam" or neglect Islamic practices. Since November 2017, for instance, the national police—controlled by the central government—has been monitoring online commentary on religion and suppressing freedom of expression when it finds such commentary "offensive to Islam."[4]

Off-screen, it has become commonplace for the police to arrest those who speak critically of Islam in public. For example, the world-renowned Turkish pianist and composer Fazil Say has been prosecuted twice because of "provocative commentary" on Islam.[5]

His crime: making gentle fun on Twitter of the Muslim call to prayer and the Muslim conception of heaven as a place where wine flows and women are the just man's reward.[6] Turkey's state-controlled television network, TRT, vilifies those who do not take part in Islamic practices. In June 2016, it hosted theologian Mustafa Askar, who said during a live broadcast that "those who don't pray in the Islamic fashion are animals."[7] Even more broadly across society, prayers of conquest at mosques for Turkey's ventures into Syria frequently boost support for Erdogan's foreign policy, while the religious content of school curricula expands yearly to help advance his right-wing Jacobin social engineering agenda.[8]

Education is at the heart of Erdogan's effort to weave sharia into Turkish society. Turkey's education system, like the police, falls under central government control, and the Ministry of Education has been pressuring citizens to conform to conservative Islamic practices in public schools. The government, for example, is formally requiring all newly built schools in Turkey to house Islamic prayer rooms.[9] In one case from 2018, an education official in Istanbul demanded that teachers bring pupils to attend morning prayers at local mosques.[10]

Perhaps nothing better illustrates Erdogan's effort to blend Islamic practices with his political power than his elevating of the Directorate of Religious Affairs—known in Turkish as the "Diyanet" and created in 1924 by Ataturk to regulate religious services in his secularist fashion. The head of the Diyanet had previously reported to a minister, but Erdogan has raised the status of the directorate's new leader, Ali Erbas, to that of a de facto vice president. Erbas now regularly attends major public events at Erdogan's side, blessing everything from Istanbul's third bridge across the Bosporus to Turkey's campaign against Kurdish groups in Syria.[11] More recently, Erbas celebrated the Azerbaijani victory in the Nagorno-Karabakh war on November 10, 2020, having prayed for this outcome beforehand.[12]

Flexing its newfound political muscle, the Diyanet has begun issuing orders to introduce sharia to Turkish society. In January 2018, the directorate released a politically nonbinding "fatwa" on its website suggesting that girls as young as nine and boys as young as twelve could marry—since, according to sharia, adulthood begins at puberty.[13] Only when the Diyanet faced a huge popular outcry did it revoke this directive—for the moment. And the next month, in February 2018, the religious body announced a new plan to appoint "Diyanet representatives" among pupils in every class of Turkey's nearly 60,000 public schools, bringing public education under the closer scrutiny of Erdogan-guided religious authorities.[14]

But those who expect Erdogan to declare Islamic law in Turkey will have to wait for quite some time. The changes he intends will not happen overnight, and will continue to play out gradually.

Using Ataturk's Tools to Dismantle His System

Having grown up in secular Turkey and faced social exclusion as a youth due to his piety and conservative views, Erdogan is motivated by deep-rooted animosity toward Ataturk's ways. And yet he has dismantled Ataturk's secularism by using the very tools that the country's founding elites provided him with: state institutions and top-down social engineering—both hallmarks of Ataturk's reforms.

But democracy poses a challenge to the current leader unknown by Ataturk. Furthermore, even as Turkey is split almost down the middle between pro- and anti-Erdogan camps, Erdogan wants to fashion this heterogeneous society in his own image. Herein lies the crisis of modern Turkey: to push forward with his platform of revolutionary change in the face of a split society, Erdogan has subverted the country's democracy.

A Consequential Leader

Erdogan will aggressively counter all efforts to vote him out both because he seeks to preserve his revolutionary changes and because he fears being prosecuted legally should he be ousted. The political movement from which he hails, National Outlook, enlists state power to Islamize a society from the top down. His conservative interpretation of Islam, applied to the Turkish government and education systems, exemplifies this approach, which has likewise undermined his opponents. French-style secularism, moreover, has ceased to govern the Turkish military and security services. Army officers, who once took oaths to defend Ataturk's secularism, now lead prayers in communal Islamic style before battle in Syria. Perhaps Erdogan feels the presence of the divine driving his success, along with a bit of Machiavellian planning.[15]

In foreign policy, Erdogan has shifted focus from Europe to immediate Middle East neighbors such as Iraq and Syria, and later beyond, intervening in the war in Libya and establishing military bases in the Indian Ocean and Persian Gulf. Nor has he shied away from conflict with Europe, occasionally bringing the EU to heel. Unlike Ataturk, who avoided European conflicts after the consolidation of Turkish independence, Erdogan seems to relish antagonizing European countries. During the 2015 Syrian refugee crisis, for instance, Erdogan carried out a successful strategy premised on opening Turkey's doors and effectively allowing the refugees to spill into European countries. To stem the crisis, Brussels was compelled to offer Erdogan a lucrative deal: cash in return for Turkey's promise to control future refugee flows into Europe.[16]

What is more, in Syria, even though Erdogan has largely relinquished his goal of ousting the regime of Bashar al-Assad, he has been deftly playing Russia and the United States, and playing the two *against each other*, to ensure Ankara has a say in Syria's future.[17]

For good or for bad, by keeping Ankara in the game from Brussels to Basra, and often channeling the voice of the Global South, Turkey's president has upgraded his country's status, and he now garners near daily attention in global news media. It is no exaggeration to say that Erdogan is Turkey's top international political brand. He has become so well-known that quite a few people around the world elide the ğ in the Turkish pronunciation of the president's surname. So, how did Erdogan—with a "silent g"—achieve his revolution, and what will be his lasting impact?

Notes

1 Professor Nora Fisher Onar, email exchange with author, February 28, 2021.

2 "Ismail Kahraman 'Zeytin Dali' Harekati Icin 'Cihat' Dedi," *Cumhuriyet*, January 26, 2018, https://www.cumhuriyet.com.tr/haber/ismail-kahraman-zeytin-dali-harekati-icin-cihat-dedi-913807.

3 Soner Cagaptay, "In Long-Secular Turkey, Sharia Is Gradually Taking Over," *Washington Post*, February 18, 2020, https://www.washingtonpost.com/news/democracy-post/wp/2018/02/16/in-long-secular-turkey-sharia-is-gradually-taking-over/.

4 "Emniyet Ozel Birim Kurdu...'Dine ve Devlete Hakaret' Edenleri Izleyecek," *Cumhuriyet*, December 4, 2017, https://www.cumhuriyet.com.tr/haber/emniyet-ozel-birim-kurdu-dine-ve-devlete-hakaret-edenleri-izleyecek-879206.

5 "Piyanist Fazil Say'in Yeniden Yargilanmasina Baslandi," *Milliyet*, May 24, 2016, https://www.milliyet.com.tr/yerel-haberler/istanbul/piyanist-fazil-say-in-yeniden-yargilanmasina-baslandi-11388518.

6 Constanze Letsch, "Turkish Composer and Pianist Convicted of

Blasphemy on Twitter," *Guardian*, April 16, 2013, https://www.
theguardian.com/world/2013/apr/15/turkish-composer-fazil-say-
convicted-blasphemhy.

7 "Prof. Dr. Mustafa Askar'in Sözlerine Inceleme," *Hurriyet*, June 14,
2016, https://www.hurriyet.com.tr/gundem/prof-dr-mustafa-askarin-
sozlerine-inceleme-40117166.

8 See Soner Cagaptay, "In Long-Secular Turkey, Sharia Is Gradually Taking
Over," *Washington Post*, February 6, 2018, https://www.washingtonpost.
com/news/democracy-post/wp/2018/02/16/in-long-secular-turkey-
sharia-is-gradually-taking-over/.

9 Zia Weise, "'Turkey's New Curriculum: More Erdogan, More Islam,"
Politico, February 13, 2017, https://www.politico.eu/article/erdogan-
turkey-education-news-coup-analysis-curriculum-history-istanbul/; and
"Yeni Okullarda Mescit Zorunlu," *A Haber*, June 25, 2017, https://www.
ahaber.com.tr/gundem/2017/06/25/yeni-okullarda-mescit-zorunlu.

10 "Ogrencilere 'Sabah Namazi' Cagrisi," January 4, 2018, https://www.
hurriyet.com.tr/egitim/ogrencilere-sabah-namazi-cagrisi-40698991.

11 See two stories from the Anadolu Agency: "Yavuz Sultan Selim Koprusu
Acildi," August 26, 2016, https://www.aa.com.tr/tr/gunun-basliklari/
yavuz-sultan-selim-koprusu-acildi/636062; and Sorwar Alam, "Special
Prayers to Be Offered for Turkish Military," January 20, 2018, https://
www.aa.com.tr/en/middle-east/special-prayers-to-be-offered-for-
turkish-military/1037106.

12 "Azerbaijan Message from Diyanet Minister Ali Erbas: Happy Victory"
(in Turkish), *Daily Sabah*, November 10, 2020, https://www.yenisafak.
com/hayat/diyanet-isleri-baskani-prof-dr-ali-erbastan-azerbaycan-
mesaji-zaferimiz-kutlu-olsun-3574542.

13 Associated Press, "Gov't Body Accused of Endorsing Marriage for Girls
from Age 9," CBS News, January 4, 2018, https://www.cbsnews.com/
news/turkey-directorate-religious-affairs-diyanet-accused-endorsing-
underage-marriage/.

14 "Religious Affairs to Assign Representatives to Universities and Schools,"
Sol International, February 9, 2018, https://news.sol.org.tr/religious-
affairs-assign-representatives-universities-and-schools-174061.

15 "Mehmetcik Afrin'de Cephede Cuma Namazini Kildi," *Sabah*, February 24, 2018.

16 Francesco Gurascio and Robin Emmott, "Declaring 'New Beginning,' EU and Turkey Seal Migrant Deal," Reuters, November 29, 2015, https://www.reuters.com/article/us-europe-migrants-turkey-idUSKBN0TI00520151130.

17 Ibid.

4

The Many Faces of Erdogan

Perhaps it is the quality all powerful politicians have in common: strength in multiple spheres. In the case of Erdogan, over and over again, he has leveraged his progress on one front to buy himself advantage on another.

The Economy Booster

Robust economic growth during the first decade of the twenty-first century, a veritable Turkish *wirtschaftswunder*, helped Erdogan build a base of adoring and loyal supporters. His popularity was not surprising given that under his rule, the country's citizens enjoyed significantly better living standards than under Kemalists for most of the twentieth century. After significant economic reforms and solid growth in the 1980s, Turkey's citizens endured at least three major recessions over a decade, the last of which, in 2000–2001, marked the country's most severe downturn since the 1970s. On the specific measure of infant mortality, before Erdogan's rise to power, Turkey's rate was comparable to that in (prewar) Syria. Now, the Turkish rate is comparable to Spain's. If the Turks used to live more like Syrians and now they live more like Spaniards, this is surely a powerful driver of Erdogan's electoral victories in over a dozen nationwide polls.

Erdogan's economic miracle also shaped Ankara's foreign policy. In Western European countries such as France and Germany, the sudden growth and prosperity following World War II instilled in citizens and policymakers a can-do attitude about foreign policy, triggering broader multilateralist political trends that eventually facilitated the creation of the EU. But Turkey's economic growth under Erdogan had perhaps the opposite effect in terms of a European connection, convincing many Turkish citizens that Ankara could stand on its own two feet in foreign policy, without relying on Europe or the West.

Subsequently, Erdogan has embraced the mantra that Turkey can restore its lost Ottoman-era greatness through a leadership position relative to Muslim-majority countries in the Middle East and beyond. During the first decade of the twenty-first century, this "soft power" initiative, driven by Ankara's newfound economic might, seemingly produced positive results. Trade boomed between Turkey and other regional states. As late as 2007, 56 percent of Turkey's trade was with Europe. By 2014, that figure was down to 42 percent. In comparison, its trade with the Middle East and North Africa increased from 13 percent in 2002 to 26 percent in 2014.[1] Ankara developed strong political ties with Middle East capitals, especially Damascus and Tehran, which Turkey's twentieth-century leaders had often ignored or antagonized.

By 2010, Turkey's clout in the Middle East appeared to be rising for the first time since the collapse of the Ottoman Empire almost a century earlier. Indeed, as the Ottoman Empire slumped into decline in the eighteenth century, the Turks tried to join the European fold as a modern country, subsumed under the continent's political framework. For at least a decade of Erdogan-led AKP rule, however, a new Turkey had awakened, founded on political stability, domestic growth, and commercial and political clout overseas, instilling a sense of imperial confidence in the Turkish people not seen perhaps since Suleiman the Magnificent ruled in the sixteenth century.[2]

The Muslim Democrat

Initially, Ankara's changing Middle East role did not produce a rift with its traditional Western allies, such as the United States. In fact, feeling boxed in by the secularist and traditionally NATO-aligned Turkish military when he took office as prime minister in early 2003, Erdogan worked to maintain good relations with Washington, while equally building ties with Middle East states. At that point particularly, he was seeking to enlist U.S. and Western support in his nearing standoff with the Turkish generals.

Although Erdogan and U.S. president George W. Bush faced a crisis following the 2003 Iraq war, when the AKP-majority parliament refused to back the American military campaign, Erdogan quickly managed to make amends by supporting U.S. efforts in Iraq and Afghanistan. By 2007–8, just as he was getting ready to take on the Turkish military brass, Erdogan was effectively Washington's darling. One senior U.S. official at the time summed up the situation like this: "U.S.-Turkish ties have never been better."[3]

Erdogan also recognized the value of the EU—and, more specifically, its core membership requirement: the subjection of an acceding country's military to civilian control. In this context, he vigorously pursued accession talks with the EU, and Ankara and Brussels commenced negotiations in 2005.

Turkey's potential to become permanently anchored in Europe unleashed an unprecedented flow of foreign direct investment— nearing 2 percent of Turkey's GDP annually—boosting its economy and Erdogan's polling numbers. In 2002, his AKP won parliamentary elections with just around one-third of the vote, thanks to the fragmented nature of his opposition. By the 2007 elections, his faction's popularity had skyrocketed to over 46 percent.

During the 2000–2010 period, Turkish politics overall looked rather rosy, and Erdogan, a refreshing and promising Turkish leader, had many outside observers concluding that he was a well-meaning politician doing the best for his people.[4] That Erdogan's brand of pious politics, which his Western observers rechristened as "Muslim democracy," represented a nonviolent alternative to al-Qaeda's version of Islam only helped underline this positive perception.[5]

The Nativist Populist

Erdogan's dark illiberalism has only become more apparent over the years, especially to those who do not follow Turkish politics daily. Specifically, he brutalizes, demonizes, and cracks down on constituencies unlikely to vote for him in order to reinforce his right-wing base.[6] This effort has entailed attacking a variety of constituencies over time, including Kemalists, liberals, secularists, leftists, social democrats, Kurdish nationalists, and Alevis—a liberal Muslim group that constitutes around 10–15 percent of the country's population.

An astute politician, Erdogan has not gone after these groups en masse. Rather, he has targeted them methodically and consecutively, undermining one group—starting with the hardline secularist Kemalists, whose power he feared most—while courting others as "allies," only to then repeat the process with the previously favored group, flipping "ally" into enemy time and time again.

Using his economic success, nativist politics, and Machiavellian strategy, Erdogan has built a base that until recently has constituted nearly half the Turkish electorate. Many of these right-wing and conservative supporters, having been lifted out of poverty by Erdogan's economic policies—which have enabled fiscal stability and attracted large amounts of foreign direct investment—practically worship Turkey's president.

But his strategy has also fueled resentment among targeted populations, whose members—including the secularists he brutalized during the Ergenekon trials (which began in 2008) and the liberals and leftists he targeted during the 2013 Gezi Park rallies (both episodes explained below)—simply detest him. This trajectory has produced deep societal polarization, throwing Turkey into a protracted crisis.

A trendsetter for twenty-first-century populism, Turkey now has among the world's most acute and advanced cases of societal polarization. When in polite dinner conversation with Turkish counterparts, it is best not to create discomfort by asking one's companions how they feel about Turkey's president. Ask them instead to compare the country before Erdogan to today's version. The counterparts will likely either respond, "Turkey was hell, and he made it heaven," or, "It was heaven, and he made it hell." A moderate or tempered response is highly unlikely.

There is nearly zero shared ground between Erdogan's supporters and his detractors, save in the under thirty-five cohort. Younger citizens seem to be embracing a more open-minded view of Turkish democracy, recognizing rights and liberties for people like themselves and people not like themselves. A study conducted by the Center for American Progress notes, "Turkey is in the midst of an important generational change; voters ages 18 to 29 represented 25 percent of the electorate in the last general election"—and this includes young conservatives who are less loyal to Erdogan and more open to Western liberal values. Excepting millennials, defined at the time of this writing as those between eighteen and forty, this mutual exclusivity of views explains why any writer who seeks to present Turkey objectively, by giving Erdogan credit where credit is due and criticizing him when criticism is warranted, will likely be subjected to character assassination attempts from both sides of the political aisle.

Many observers are deeply worried about Turkey's polarization, but Erdogan thrives on it. He does, however, have one genuine cause for concern: Fethullah Gulen, a Turkish Muslim cleric who lives in the United States and directs an Islamist movement from afar.

Notes

1 Soner Cagaptay, *The Rise of Turkey: The Twenty-First Century's Muslim Power* (Potomac, 2014), 5.

2 Ibid., 15.

3 As reported by senior Turkish diplomat, correspondence with author, January 3, 2019.

4 "A Turkish Success Story," *New York Times*, January 28, 2004, https://www.nytimes.com/2004/01/28/opinion/a-turkish-success-story.html.

5 Helene Cooper, "America Seeks Bonds to Islam, Obama Insists," *New York Times*, April 6, 2009, https://www.nytimes.com/2009/04/07/world/europe/07prexy.html?em.

6 Soner Cagaptay, *The New Sultan: Erdogan and the Crisis of Modern Turkey* (London: I.B. Tauris, 2017).

5

Erdogan's Worst Enemy?

Almost without fail, during my lectures around the United States, an audience member will stand up and ask me what I think of "Fethullah Gulen, the poor cleric who lives in Pennsylvania and who has been opposing Erdogan." I respond that only one part of this question is factually correct: Gulen does live in Pennsylvania. For nearly a decade, Erdogan and Gulen were allies, with the political-religious network leader helping the Turkish president intimidate his opposition, undermine democratic institutions and checks and balances, and push aside the Kemalist military. But in recent years, a deep rift has formed between them.

When Erdogan became prime minister in 2003, his deepest fears involved the secularist Turkish armed forces and the measures generals would take to undermine him. After all, the military had a record of coups and interference against elected governments in Turkey since the 1960s and, more recently, against a government that included political Islamists.

In 1997, the military had orchestrated protests against the Welfare Party (known as Refah), a political Islamist faction to which Erdogan then belonged. The generals forced Refah out of government in a series of events later dubbed the Postmodern Coup. Two years thereafter, Turkey's Constitutional Court, a Kemalist institution then in alliance with the military, banned the party on grounds that its policies violated the country's secularist charter.

Following the ban, Refah cadres established a new faction called the Virtue Party (FP, or Fazilet), which itself was shut down by the Constitutional Court in 2001. Realizing that Turkey's secularist elites would always combat political Islamist parties, Erdogan split from the latter, forming his Justice and Development Party and branding it as a "nonpolitical Islamist" faction espousing "conservative democratic" values.[1]

Erdogan knew he had a chance to convince his Western observers, but not the secularist generals and their allies in Turkey, that he had jettisoned political Islam. Therefore, actual power seemed elusive for him, even as he took office as the country's prime minister.

Enter Gulen, with his power-hungry followers serving in the country's bureaucracy and media. Erdogan viewed Gulen as a useful ally. And Gulen, who had established his political-religious network in the 1970s and had his own run-ins with the secularist Turkish military, wanted more access to power himself. As a religious-brotherhood-cum-political movement, the Gulen network had been placing its members in influential positions in government, creating a self-serving ladder of political ascent for its followers.

Accordingly, Gulen was more than eager to help Erdogan against the military, but his motives were naturally not at all altruistic. Gulen knew he would benefit greatly from supporting Turkey's new and popular prime minister. His alliance with Erdogan promised to multiply Gulen's power through a much-wanted prize: an opportunity to place even more Gulen followers and sympathizers in key positions in the country's bureaucracy, courts, and national police force, but—more important—eventually the military.

In addition to their political and ideological motives, Gulen and Erdogan shared a common trauma only a few years old, and similarly inflicted on both by the Kemalist military and the courts. Erdogan had been Istanbul's mayor in 1997 during the Postmodern Coup. And, as discussed earlier, in 1998 the courts convicted him for reciting a poem said to violate Turkey's secularist constitution. He thereafter eschewed political Islam, at least in his rhetoric. Even after becoming prime minister, Erdogan never forgot how the generals and their judicial allies had mistreated him.

Gulen's run-in occurred in 1999, when the courts charged him with "founding an organization with the goal of replacing the secular state with one founded on religious rules."[2] That same year, he left Turkey for the United States for medical treatment. All along, he remained spiteful toward the generals and their allies in Turkey, often broadcasting videos targeting the military.[3] His movement also worked tirelessly to place members into the Turkish military officer corps, developing a presence in sensitive branches such as personnel management, education, and intelligence, where they would build a resilient network to prevent military action against the movement and to undermine opponents.[4]

Hence, the Gulen-Erdogan alliance blossomed after 2003, with each man benefiting significantly from it. Erdogan, as anticipated, appointed many of Gulen's followers and sympathizers to key positions in the police and state prosecutor's offices, among other places in government. In turn, Gulen's movement emerged as a formidable force in Turkey over the coming years.

Gulen then did his part to help Erdogan. In 2008, Erdogan-appointed and Gulen-aligned prosecutors and police launched a series of court cases, collectively dubbed Ergenekon, alleging an imminent coup plot against Erdogan. That the military had recently issued a stern and ill-considered warning to Erdogan on its website, dubbed the "e-coup," was cited as evidence of the allegation.[5]

Gulen-owned media, such as the daily *Zaman*, played a crucial role in propagating the coup charges, while simultaneously painting Erdogan as a democrat fighting against the elites and a nefarious "deep state." (Thus, a nontraditional term came into common use, and was later adopted as a favorite of the Trump administration and populist leaders elsewhere.)

The prosecutors could not produce a convincing account of this coup—much of the so-called evidence was concocted—but they used the allegations to lock up nearly a quarter of active-duty generals and hundreds of other high-ranking officers in the military.[6]

Gulen-aligned police and prosecutors also started targeting, intimidating, and jailing other members of the "deep state," including Erdogan's secular civil society opponents. Even veteran journalists who covered the Ergenekon case, such as Ahmet Sik, were targeted. Sik was arrested for rebutting the claimed coup plot and targeting the Gulen movement.

Some others, assessing the military to be the greater threat to democracy than was Erdogan, also allied with the prime minister and Gulen during this period. For instance, *Taraf*, a self-professed liberal daily, fiercely denigrated almost anyone who opposed Erdogan and Gulen.

When Sik, a fellow journalist, was arrested, *Taraf*'s editors ran a front-page story saying, "[Sik and his colleagues taken into custody] were not doing journalism." More than a few liberals, including *Taraf* editor Ahmet Altan, hopped on the Erdogan-Gulen bandwagon, hoping to use it to undermine the military's role in Turkish politics, but unwittingly helping Erdogan and Gulen emerge as feared figures in the country.[7]

In the current century, democracy in Turkey first came under attack in 2008, eight years before the failed coup attempt, when Gulen (joined by the aforementioned liberals) helped Erdogan construct a "republic of fear" in which opposing Erdogan through ideas became a crime—punishable by jail. A number of prominent Turkish intellectuals and civil society activists, including Turkan Saylan, who ran an NGO promoting girls' secular education, and Ahmet Sik, the journalist who investigated the Gulen movement, were jailed during the Ergenekon trials, sending shock waves across Turkish society, and also serving as warning shots that opposing Gulen and Erdogan had consequences.

Erdogan's (and Gulen's) strategy of intimidation worked, driving up levels of fear among his opponents. Then came the straw that broke the camel's back: the top brass of the Turkish military resigned en masse in July 2011, appearing to signal Erdogan's (and Gulen's) immutable power.[8]

In the meantime, of course, Gulen was busy getting ready for his final showdown with Erdogan and everyone else in Turkey. Gulen's movement, known to its members as Hizmet (The Service), encompasses a highly secretive network. According to veteran Turkish journalist Sedat Ergin, Gulen used the 2008 Ergenekon trials to airdrop his supporters into key strategic positions in the military, which were left vacant by purged secularist officers.[9] These Gulen-aligned officers, many of whom had risen to become one- and two-star generals by 2016, served as the central processing unit of the coup plot against Erdogan—using trumped-up coup charges and the witch hunt in 2008 to eliminate secular officers standing in their way of carrying out an actual coup in 2016. One might consider this the ultimate example of Turkey as a figurative onion.

"Doner Kebab Master"

The generals were smart to throw in the towel, having just lost their key ally: the high courts. A referendum Erdogan won in September 2010, with support from *Taraf, Zaman,* and other Gulen-backed or supporting outlets, had changed the country's constitution, giving Erdogan the power to appoint a majority of judges to high courts without a confirmation process. The courts now belonged to Erdogan, a development that drew little international pushback or attention.

The EU, which later would crack down on Polish leader Jaroslaw Kaczynski's efforts to stack the Warsaw courts with his handpicked judges, appeared unbothered by Erdogan's similar efforts. In the case of Turkey, for around a decade Brussels appeared to be paying lip service to a simplistic, Manichean viewpoint: Erdogan the Good versus "nefarious secular Turkish elites."[10]

This view was especially ironic since Erdogan was then also borrowing from Russian president Vladimir Putin's playbook, intimidating newspapers and networks and the secular- or liberal-minded owners of these outlets through politically motivated tax audits. This instrument helped him send warning shots not only to the press, but also to large businesses, to move immediately out of his way or else bow to his power.

The lethal blow to the press came from Erdogan's own intricate process of media monopolization, which very few outside Turkey were willing to narrate beyond providing the rosy picture of Erdogan then prevalent in the United States and European capitals. Around 2010–11, a near-global chorus mistakenly adulated Erdogan's party as Turkey's democratic force.[11]

In actuality, a different plot was unfolding, led by Erdogan. In a repeated scenario, the government media watchdog would confiscate an independent outlet, which would then—as a prominent newspaper editor explained at the time[12]—be sold in a single-bidder auction to an Erdogan supporter, without fail in a transaction funded by loans from a public bank. The newspapers and networks, such as Sabah and ATV, soon caved to Erdogan, shifting their editorial line. Ironically, while most international media were praising Erdogan for making Turkey supposedly "more liberal," Erdogan was busy taking control of the press.[13]

With the strongest link in his opposition—the military—politically neutralized, and the courts, media, and businesses falling under his sway, Erdogan felt free to go after other societal groups, his "allies," ranging from social democrats to liberals, for whom he had never really cared much. In his earlier years in power, he had left these groups to their own devices—excepting Alevis, whose liberal interpretation of Islam often makes them a target of political Islamists—providing them with a false sense of security. Erdogan's hardening social conservatism after 2010–11—for instance, his insistence that all women should have three children and his insistence on promoting religious schools—soon ended this illusion.[14]

A coalition of civil society groups, including Alevis from the left and conservatives from the right, rose up against Erdogan in 2013 during Istanbul's Gezi Park rallies, which were sparked by a plan to build a shopping center in a green space but soon widened to encompass a larger scope of grievances. In retaliation, Erdogan carried out a massive and bloody crackdown. His suppression worked not only because the police, under his control, acted as effective storm troopers, but also because large groups of Kurdish nationalists eventually abstained, hoping that their passivity would help ongoing government peace talks with the Kurdistan Workers Party (PKK). In 2015, when these talks collapsed, Kurdish nationalists rose up against Erdogan, but he crushed them, also jailing their charismatic and capable leader, Peoples' Democratic Party chair Selahattin Demirtas, the first party leader able to broaden the HDP's base to include non-Kurdish nationalist voters.

Now to the metaphor: Erdogan proved himself something of a "doner kebab master" in evading a Western critique of his undermining of Turkish democracy. Doner kebab, or "gyro" in English, is meat on a spit, cut by the master in almost paper-thin slices. If patrons do not watch closely, they really will not see the kebab shrinking. In this same way, Erdogan's undermining of Turkish democratic institutions is not a product of just the last few years. He has been slicing away at them for a long time. But his incremental approach prevented a broader global reaction until the massive crackdown on the Gezi demonstrators. For some, a closer look did not come until three years later, when coup plotters failed to oust him on a July evening in 2016.

Allies into Enemies

The mass resignation of the Turkish military's top brass in 2011 threw the self-serving nature of the Erdogan-Gulen relationship into the open, setting in motion events that culminated in the 2016 coup attempt in which Gulen-aligned military officers would play a key role. These events have fundamentally changed Turkey, its foreign policy, and global perceptions of Erdogan.

The Erdogan-Gulen alliance dissolved swiftly. After 2011, each man wanted to run Turkey single-handedly, catalyzing a raw power struggle. In December 2013, Gulen-aligned police and prosecutors pressed corruption allegations against Erdogan and his family members, leaking illegally taped conversations between Erdogan and his son Bilal, among others, to the public.[15] Erdogan demoted and arrested these prosecutors and police, while also purging, arresting, and harassing Gulenists nationwide serving in a range of government agencies. The Gulen movement's countermove: the bold, if ill-advised, coup attempt.

According to an interpretation of Sigmund Freud's "narcissism of small differences" theory, the more similar two people are, the more they hate each other after a falling-out. This theory regarding relations between neighbors, when applied to the Erdogan-Gulen relationship, perhaps helps explain the intensification of their mutual animosity after 2011, and even more so after 2016; the two men are said to loathe each other more than they do any other political actors in Turkey.

Erdogan was saved from the coup attempt because he was on

vacation outside Ankara at the time. And although the coup failed in the end, the putschists, strategically concentrated in the national air force, still managed to bomb the Turkish capital. Taking into account that Ankara had last come under direct military attack in 1402, when the Turco-Mongol conqueror Tamerlane's armies occupied it, the coup attempt shocked and traumatized the country, including constituencies not vehemently against Erdogan.

An equally dramatic impact of the failed coup has been its role in shaping Turkey's foreign policy orientation. Together with developments linked to the Syrian war, and aided by Putin's shrewd moves, post-coup events have steered Ankara away from the United States and into the outer orbit of its historical nemesis, Russia.

Notes

1 Karl Vick, "Secular Democrat or Zealot?" *Washington Post*, November 10, 2002, https://www.washingtonpost.com/archive/politics/2002/11/10/secular-democrat-or-zealot/895c46b0-eee2-44f4-9081-a47161a852a0/.

2 "U.S. Charter Schools Tied to Powerful Turkish Imam," CBS News, May 13, 2020, https://www.cbsnews.com/news/us-charter-schools-tied-to-powerful-turkish-imam/3/.

3 "Fetullah Gulen DGM Dosyasi," court document, T. C. Ankara Devlet Guvenlik Mahkemesi Cumhuriyet Bassavciligi.

4 Firat Kozok, "Gulen Infiltrated Turkey's Military for Decades, Ucok Says," Bloomberg, August 2, 2016, https://www.bloombergquint.com/politics/gulen-infiltrated-turkey-military-for-decades-prosecutor-says.

5 "Army 'Concerned' by Turkey Vote," BBC News, April 28, 2007, http://news.bbc.co.uk/2/hi/europe/6602375.stm. Also see Dexter Filkins, "Turkey's Thirty-Year Coup," *The New Yorker*, October 10, 2016, https://www.newyorker.com/magazine/2016/10/17/turkeys-thirty-year-coup.

6   Gareth Jenkins, "The Ergenekon Verdicts: Chronicle of an Injustice Foretold," *Turkey Analyst* 6 no. 14 (2013), http://www.turkeyanalyst.org/publications/turkey-analyst-articles/item/50. Also see Gareth Jenkins, *Between Fact and Fantasy: Turkey's Ergenekon Investigation* (Washington DC: Central Asia Institute/Silk Road Studies Program, 2009), https://www.silkroadstudies.org/resources/pdf/SilkRoadPapers/2009_08_SRP_Jenkins_Turkey-Ergenekon.pdf, and Dani Rodrik, "Ergenekon and Sledgehammer: Building or Undermining the Rule of Law?" Turkish Policy Quarterly, May, 11, 2011, https://www.hks.harvard.edu/publications/ergenekon-and-sledgehammer-building-or-undermining-rule-law#citation.

7   "Ahmet Altan: Nedim Sener ve Ahmet Sik Tutuklandiginda Taraf ne Yazmisti, Ahmet Hakan Hangi Yalani Atiyor?" T24, May 19, 2016, https://t24.com.tr/haber/sampiyon-besiktas-sezonu-yenilgiyle-kapatti,341111.

8   Adam Martin, "Turkey's Military Chiefs Resign En Masse," *Atlantic*, July 29, 2011, https://www.theatlantic.com/international/archive/2011/07/turkeys-military-chiefs-resign-en-masse/353457/.

9   Barcin Yinanc, "Ample Evidence to Prove that Gulenists Were Behind Turkey's Coup Attempt: Journalist Sedat Ergin," *Hurriyet Daily News*, August 28, 2017, https://www.hurriyetdailynews.com/ample-evidence-to-prove-that-gulenists-were-behind-turkeys-coup-attempt-journalist-sedat-ergin-117241.

10 "EU Court Orders Halt to Polish Judicial Overhaul; Leader Says to Appeal," Reuters, October 19, 2018, https://mobile.reuters.com/article/amp/idUSKCN1MT1O9.

11 "Is Turkey Turning Its Back on the West?" *Economist*, October 21, 2010, https://www.economist.com/leaders/2010/10/21/is-turkey-turning-its-back-on-the-west.

12 Turkish newspaper editor, discussion with author.

13 "Erdogan Pulls It Off," *Economist,* September 13, 2010, https://www.economist.com/newsbook/2010/09/13/erdogan-pulls-it-off.

14 "Erdogan: En az Uc Cocuk Dogurun," *Hurriyet*, March 7, 2008, https://www.hurriyet.com.tr/gundem/erdogan-en-az-uc-cocuk-dogurun-8401981.

15 Mark Lowen, "Turkey's Erdogan Battles 'Parallel State,'" BBC News, December 17, 2014, https://www.bbc.com/news/world-europe-30492348.

6

How Putin Won Erdogan's Heart— and How Obama Lost It

Turkey's recent move toward Russia constitutes a sea change, even compared to geopolitical dynamics from a decade ago. Many years earlier, at the outset of the Cold War, Turkey anchored itself in the West by seeking formal ties with the United States and Western European countries. These efforts were driven in large part by historical Turkish fears of Russia, exacerbated by Stalin's threats against Turkish territory and sovereignty during and after World War II under the guise of advancing communism. Together with Ataturk's vision of pivoting to "contemporary civilization," which the Kemalists defined as Europe, postwar fears of Russia resulted in Turkey's joining the Council of Europe in 1950 and NATO in 1952, starting a process of closer alignment between Ankara and the West.

Ankara on occasion still sought deeper ties with non-Western states, such as in the 1980s when Prime Minister Turgut Ozal cultivated the country's Middle East neighbors as trade partners in order to spread Turkish influence regionally. Ozal had some success in this regard, but the regional ties did not come at the expense of Ankara's relations with the West. Overall, Ankara's bonds with the United States and Europe, including the eastern part of the continent after the fall of communism, dominated Turkish foreign policy—until the rise of Erdogan.

Erdogan, too, turned to Europe after coming to power, although only to then drop it as excess political weight. During the initial years of his rule, he instrumentalized the EU-accession process in order to curb the Kemalist generals' political power in Ankara. In 2004, he passed legislation "to qualify Ankara for EU accession," eliminating the dominant role of the military in the Turkish National Security Council.[1] This development laid the legal groundwork for his eventual showdown with the generals during the 2008 Ergenekon trials. It was not surprising, therefore, that once he sidelined the generals in 2011, Erdogan basically lost interest in EU accession.

But both sides deserve blame for Turkey's pivot away from the EU. By creating obstacles, such as firmer opening and closing criteria for each of the more than thirty membership discussion "rounds" (i.e., chapters) with new candidates and unanimous-consent approval by all twenty-seven EU members (twenty-eight, with Croatia's 2013 accession)—obstacles often backed by key Union members, such as France and Germany—Brussels provided an alibi for Ankara to turn away from Europe.[2] Not surprisingly, while Croatia, which started accession talks alongside Turkey in 2005, deservedly became an EU member, Turkey's membership prospects dimmed, with numerous accession chapters soon deemed unopenable by France and other member countries. These faltering EU hopes helped encourage Erdogan's focus on the Middle East.

By the 2010s, the Turkish-EU relationship was no longer about common values and a shared destiny, but was focused instead on transactional deals often marred by disputes. A case in point was the 2015 "Turkish-EU crisis," when Ankara's open-door refugee policy, threatening Europe, drew a promise of cash from EU leaders in return for controlling future refugee flows. A similar Turkish attempt in early 2020 provides evidence that the future of Turkish-EU ties will be far from smooth.[3]

The other relationship anchoring Turkey to the West—ties with the United States—also came unmoored in the 2010s, owing to developments related to the Arab uprisings. These events produced even more dramatic outcomes for Turkish foreign policy. At the start of the uprisings, in 2011–12—encouraged by his success in having pushed aside the traditionally pro-NATO Turkish military and basking in his country's recent economic boom—Erdogan felt free to launch a more independent foreign policy than before. He unveiled regional and Middle East power initiatives—acting independently from the United States, and then increasingly breaking with Washington when necessary. His apparent goal: to make Turkey a standalone power in the Middle East. According to this vision, dubbed "strategic depth" and articulated by Erdogan's foreign minister Ahmet Davutoglu, who later served as prime minister, Turkey could rise as a regional and then global power only if it built ties with its Muslim-majority neighbors equal in strength to its ties with the United States and Europe.[4] Turkey could then naturally stand on its own as a world actor, without having to always rely upon—and subsequently listen to—Washington and Brussels.

Moreover, no longer feeling confined by the Kemalist military and foreign policy elites who had nurtured Turkey's ties with Israel, Erdogan conveniently ruptured historical Turkish-Israeli ties—Turkey having been the first Muslim-majority state to recognize Israel, in 1949. In spring 2010, a supply flotilla manned by pro-Palestinian and pro-Hamas NGO figures, and tacitly blessed by Erdogan—despite Israeli warnings that the gesture would result in a military response—set sail from Turkish ports to "deliver aid to Gaza."

In light of the predictable outcome, Erdogan had effectively set a trap involving his nationals. On May 31, 2010, the Israeli military boarded the *Mavi Marmara* vessel in international Mediterranean waters near its territory and killed nine Turkish civilians. In response, Erdogan suspended all military and diplomatic ties between Ankara and Jerusalem. Despite the sharp tensions—or perhaps because of them—the Turkish leader may at that moment have foreseen a breezy future; his dream of navigating Ankara away from the West, and toward the Muslim-majority Middle East, seemed assured. In speeches thereafter, Erdogan declared himself the authority over the unfolding events, which he cast in an international rather than Turkish nationalist context.[5]

"Muslim Brotherhood Lite" Meets the Real Thing

In 2011–12, Ankara's (and Erdogan's) fortunes indeed appeared to be rising across the Middle East. From Egypt to Tunisia, the Muslim Brotherhood was ascending to positions of power, giving Erdogan an opening to make calls in the region. With Turkey's economy having experienced nearly a decade of strong growth and the country's soft power rising in the Middle East, analyses by scholars, including some by this author, appeared suggesting that Turkey could rise as a regional power[6]—if Erdogan played his hand well, consolidating democracy at home to end Turkey's crippling societal polarization, but also making the country a model power across the Middle East, employing smart statecraft.[7] Turkey indeed seemed a hopeful case when viewed from the Middle East. According to one Arab observer, Turkey was a model for Egyptians and other Arabs because it "looked like their country culturally, it looked like Europe economically, it simply worked!"[8]

In this regard, developments in Egypt were especially important, serving as a primer on how to get things wrong. The largest Arab country by population, Egypt can make Arab cultural and social trends hegemonic by adopting them. After the fall of President Hosni Mubarak in 2011, Erdogan quickly moved to build influence in Cairo, and in quick succession in additional regional capitals, by embracing parties aligned with the Muslim Brotherhood.

The Brotherhood, founded in Egypt by Hassan al-Banna in 1928, has had limited ideological or political influence in Turkey. Turkish Islamism generally traces its roots to Sufi sects (Naqshbandi, Bektashi, and Qadiriyah) or their derivatives, such as the Nurcu, Iskenderpasa, and Ismailaga movements. In terms of its political branding, though, Erdogan's AKP might also be regarded as "Muslim Brotherhood lite"—because there is significant overlap in the political programs, specifically in creating space for Islam in national politics. Erdogan shared a common opponent with Brotherhood branches in Arab countries—authoritarian political cultures intent on suppressing political Islam, rooted in royal or military institutions. So, while the AKP's roots lie not in the Muslim Brotherhood but in the uniquely Turkish Milli Gorus movement—in which Erdogan learned politics in the 1970s[9]—Milli Gorus has ideological similarities to the Brotherhood, despite the lack of proven organizational ties.[10]

Kinship with the Brotherhood seduced Erdogan politically, convincing him to full-heartedly support the short-lived government led by Brotherhood member Mohamed Morsi (r. 2012–13). Erdogan subsequently won great influence in Cairo, but following Morsi's ouster by Gen. Abdul Fattah al-Sisi, the Turkish leader completely lost his Egyptian gains—almost overnight. Nearly simultaneously in Syria and Libya, more radical factions overran the Brotherhood. Erdogan's continued support for the Brotherhood in Egypt put Ankara at odds with key Gulf Cooperation Council members, especially Saudi Arabia and the United Arab Emirates, as well as Israel, which view the group—in the case of Israel, the Brotherhood's Palestinian offshoot, Hamas—as their greatest domestic threat and regional challenge.

In hindsight, perhaps no one could have guessed that the Brotherhood would rise and fall so quickly. In some cases—such as with the Iraqi Islamic Party—Erdogan adjusted quickly, diversifying his outreach to include the Masoud Barzani–led Kurdish Democratic Party and the country's Shia political leaders. In other cases, Erdogan's bet on Brotherhood-linked parties failed. Investment in multiple competitors, especially Morsi's opponents in the Egyptian instance, would certainly have made for a more durable regional imprint. By early 2021, the overall impact of Erdogan's Brotherhood policy in the Middle East was that—contrary to his vision in 2011—Ankara had nearly no friends among Arab-majority states, with the exception of Qatar and Libya's internationally backed, Tripoli-based government.

Syrian Affair

By 2015, Erdogan's Syria policy had also put Ankara at odds with the Assad regime and its main patrons, Iran and Russia. In particular, the November 2015 incident in which Turkey shot down a Russian military aircraft that briefly violated Turkey's airspace from Syria exposed Ankara to the vagaries of its historical nemesis.

What is more, events in Syria caused U.S.-Turkish ties to zigzag. In 2013, President Barack Obama eschewed a military option even after Assad used chemical weapons against the rebels—a move that apparently crossed Obama's stated redline—prompting Ankara to take a go-it-alone military stance against Damascus, with the hope Washington would eventually follow suit. But this wish remained unrequited, given Obama's resistance to entering a war in a Muslim-majority country. Erdogan had failed to read the U.S. president correctly, with grave ramifications for Turkey's Syria policy and later U.S.-Turkish ties.[11]

Simultaneously, Ankara started allowing aspirant foreign fighters to cross its border into Syria. This policy gave rise to speculation that Erdogan quietly supported the Islamic State, but in fact he did not. Between 2011 and 2014, Erdogan saw little risk that allowing volunteers to go fight Assad would result in a metastasizing terrorist network that could reach back into Turkey, Europe, and even the United States. He was not alone in this underestimation. To assert the opposite is to substitute for evidence the suspicion that Erdogan is both uniquely capable and uniquely culpable or, as I call it, "*reductio ad Erdoganum.*"[12] This tendency, observable in both directions and evident since Erdogan's rise in 2003, reflects a broader distillation by European and U.S. analysts of the Turkish scene to pro- or anti-Erdogan passions. Adulation often prevailed in the first decade of his rule, loathing and disdain in the second. In truth, overpraise led to the fallacy that Erdogan was a democrat, when in fact he was creating a republic of fear; demonization led unfairly to his mislabeling as a friend of the Islamic State (IS).[13]

In allowing radicals to cross into Syria, Erdogan appears to have believed that his preferred factions—linked to the Muslim Brotherhood—would take over, eventually vanquishing the jihadists. But he was mistaken on multiple levels. At least some of those who crossed into Syria have morphed into IS fighters, and without U.S. support, the Turkish-backed factions could never become powerful enough to oust Assad or defeat his formidable patrons, Russia and Iran.

Even worse, and signaling the further failure of Erdogan's Syria strategy, the jihadists successfully swept across Syria, declaring their caliphate in 2014 and carrying out attacks across Europe and the United States, from Paris in 2015 to Nice and Orlando in 2016.[14] All along, Ankara remained focused on Assad, as if trying to wish away the Islamic State.

Kurdish Troubles

Obama, for his part, struggled to gain timely support from Ankara to combat the Islamic State, even while resisting bids to send U.S. ground troops to Syria.[15] The American quest for an anti-jihadist ally led to the Syria-based People's Defense Units (YPG), a Kurdish group linked to the Turkey-based Kurdistan Workers Party (PKK), which is designated as a terrorist organization by Turkey, the United States, and other NATO members.

The YPG, whose Marxist-Leninist pedigree naturally leads it to oppose religion and jihadism, was more than eager to fight the Islamic State in return for tacit U.S. recognition of the PKK offshoot. This was especially true after the YPG folded itself under the umbrella Syrian Democratic Forces in 2015, allowing Washington to arm this group without the legal trace of arming the PKK. The deal appeared messy, but it was too good for Obama to pass up. Ankara never agreed to Obama's evolving policy of partnering with the YPG to fight the Islamic State, and this issue soon reached a near breaking point for U.S.-Turkish ties. Signaling Ankara's objection to this policy, Turkish foreign minister Mevlut Cavusoglu frequently criticizes the United States for its "support to and collaboration with the YPG," saying that as far as Ankara is concerned, this is akin to Washington working with the PKK.[16]

At the time in 2015, Erdogan was feeling rattled by the rise of the pro–Kurdish nationalist and progressive Peoples' Democratic Party alliance in Turkey, which—running on a joint list in the June elections—had denied Erdogan's AKP a legislative majority for the first time in thirteen years. That summer, the combination of growing U.S. support for the YPG and growing assertiveness by the HDP strengthened Erdogan's conviction to take whatever steps were necessary to stop Kurdish nationalist success at home and in the near-abroad.

Coupled with rising Turkish popular animus toward the PKK, Obama's YPG policy served to deeply undermine the relationship between the two leaders and their countries, even as it eventually registered successes in degrading the Islamic State.

Enter the Russian Nemesis

Complicating matters for the worse, near simultaneous developments in Syria shifted the longstanding balance in U.S.-Turkish-Russian ties. For Turkey, fears of the Russian threat date to the Ottoman era. At one point or another, the Ottoman Turks ruled over or conclusively defeated all of modern Turkey's neighbors—all except Russia. Between the reign of Catherine the Great in the eighteenth century, when the Ottoman and Russian Empires became neighbors, and the 1917 Russian Revolution, the two empires fought nearly a dozen long wars, most of them instigated—and won—by Russia.

With good reason, then, most Turkish elites have increasingly been keen to avoid escalation against Russia unless they have Western backing. In its long history of confrontation with Russia, Turkey and its Ottoman predecessor have generally lost when going it alone; durable victories came only during the Crimean War of 1853–56 with British and French assistance, and during the Cold War with U.S. support.

Erdogan missed this point in 2012 when he interfered in Syria's civil war against the Assad regime without securing long-term U.S. support. When in September 2015 Putin deployed his military forces to help Assad, it was not a matter of if but when Turkish and Russian forces, operating against each other, would have a run-in and Ankara would be left effectively on its own. The feared scenario took place months later, in November 2015, when the Turkish air force shot down a Russian plane that had briefly violated Turkish airspace. Putin reacted harshly, slapping tourism- and trade-related sanctions on Turkey, launching intense bombing raids against opposition groups tied to Turkey, and threatening to fire at any Turkish forces inside Syria.[17] The last of these threats undermined Ankara-backed rebels seeking to challenge Assad's forces.

At the same time, Putin's economic sanctions, which included a ban on Russian tourists to Turkey and an import prohibition covering many Turkish goods, suggested a possibly "nuclear impact" on Turkey's economy and Erdogan's constituents. Russia is the number-one tourist source for Turkey—in 2015, more than 3.5 million visited the country.[18] Key businesses targeted by Putin's sanctions, such as large food exporters and construction companies, happen to encompass Erdogan's major supporters. Still another, more terrifying option may have been under consideration, with one official suggesting that the Russians had simulated a nuclear attack against Istanbul, although mainly as a way to scare the Turkish leadership.[19]

In its immediate response to this building threat, Ankara requested to buy Patriot missiles from Washington to defend its southern border with Syria against Russia. President Obama, not eager to bring the United States into a conflict with Russia—but also unable to meet Turkish demands on price and the technology transfer required for the Patriot system—declined, leaving Erdogan on his own. By early 2016, it looked as if the eighteenth Russian-Turkish war could start, and the Turks did not see odds in their favor.

The Coup Plot That Changed Everything Between Erdogan and Putin

Following the summer 2016 coup attempt, Putin, rather unexpectedly, reached out to Erdogan, seeking to build a connection based on shared alienation with Washington and the West. To understand the Russian leader's motives, one must look to his perception of the Cold War. Whereas as standard histories date its end to 1991, with the fall of the Soviet Union, Putin views the Cold War as being very much alive, now in its second phase. This time, Russia is playing to win—here, by pitting Turkey against the United States, thereby dividing NATO.

Thus, instead of further marginalizing Erdogan following the putsch attempt, Putin embraced him.

Washington, however, tended to fall prey to *"reductio ad Erdoganum."*[20] To this day, in my talks in Washington and Europe, the absolutely most popular question involves whether Erdogan staged the 2016 coup attempt himself. To which I answer: even he is not that good.

Moreover, nearly without exception, every successful coup worldwide in recent memory has been launched in the dead of night, around three in the morning, when the streets are empty. Citizens generally object to military rule, and generals know their takeover can succeed *only* if it is viewed as a fait accompli. By the time the populace awakens to tanks on the streets, it has no true path to reverse the outcome. This was the plan of the Turkish coup plotters, who saw an additional opportunity in Erdogan's being on vacation that day, away from Ankara and therefore unable to coordinate a response.

But a number of problems conspired to upset the coup's success. To begin with, whereas the central processing unit almost certainly consisted of Gulen-aligned officers, the lower-level and side operatives included an assortment of opportunists lured by promises of powerful positions afterward, secularists who hated Erdogan more than they hated Gulen, and foot soldiers who believed they were following legitimate orders—a flimsy grouping that risked unraveling at the first instance of trouble.

And trouble was quick to surface: Turkish intelligence appears to have learned about the coup attempt during the early hours of July 15. (The question remains of whether Putin had a role in informing Erdogan.) Military elements opposed to the putsch thus began aggressively planning countermeasures. With their plot outed, the putschists had two options: act earlier in the evening, and perhaps succeed, or risk arrest by carrying out the original plan. They opted for the former, launching at around 10 p.m. on Friday July 15. Anyone who has spent a summer evening stalled in Istanbul's chaotic traffic can tell you that this timing was hardly auspicious. And Turkish citizens took to the streets en masse—both supporters of Erdogan and his opponents. The coup instigators were unable to mobilize any popular support.[21] Nobody, it turns out, wanted to live under military rule in twenty-first century Turkey.

Istanbul is a city of fifteen million residents (more, by unofficial counts) spread over two continents, separated by the Bosporus Strait. Residents cross from one side to the other on ferries and subways, but car traffic over the city's three suspension bridges is notorious. On a Friday evening, many secular Istanbullus are out on the town, dining late, drinking, whereas many religious residents are returning from prayer at the mosque, which ends around 9:30 in summer. The resulting auto traffic thus was critical in foiling the plot—as early as 7:30, major traffic congestion was reported along the two major Bosporus bridges.[22]

Putin grasped, early on, the illegitimate and unpopular nature of the coup plot. Any hesitation or equivocation on this matter, he saw, would be interpreted as support for coups and as a dismissal of Turkish popular opinion. Ironically, many in the West, including Ankara's NATO allies, failed to see this reality. Their agnosticism over the plot was driven by bitterness toward Erdogan and distaste for his policies, from his democratic transgressions at home to his actions in Syria. Well-wishing calls from Turkey's Western allies therefore took days in some cases, or even weeks, to materialize. With the exception of Britain, Turkey's key NATO allies in Europe delayed their outreach to Erdogan. The U.S. government issued a statement within hours of the plot, but Erdogan was waiting specifically for Obama's immediate phone call, which did not come. Indeed, when Washington did call, four days after the event, the U.S. official on the other line was Secretary of State John Kerry, not Obama.

Putin the Great

This was Putin's moment. The Russian leader was sharply aware that because Gulen lived in the United States, many in Turkey would be immediately inclined to blame Washington for the putsch attempt. In fact, this is what many in Erdogan's inner circle did right away, with Bekir Bozdag, then Turkish minister of justice, insinuating that Washington and NATO had both known what was coming—and did nothing.[23]

Putin not only was the first world leader to reach out to Erdogan, but he also invited the Turkish president to Saint Petersburg for consultations. Just imagine Erdogan's relief: not only were his troubles with Putin being alleviated, but he was effectively being offered Russian protection. One Turkish journalist even suggested that Putin may have proposed to send Russian special forces stationed on a Greek island to help Erdogan quiet any residual coup rumblings.[24] Never mind that no Russian soldiers were likely even based on a Greek isle—the sentiment was what counted. Putin wanted to be a source of consolation, and to parlay Erdogan's gratitude to Russia's geopolitical advantage.

Erdogan's Russia visit occurred on August 9—notably to the imperial capital, not Moscow. Putin gave Erdogan a "czar's welcome" at the Konstantinovsky Palace, built by Catherine the Great, among the first Russian leaders to establish a trend of brutalizing the Ottoman Turks. Putin's message to Erdogan was clear: while his historical predecessor Catherine the Great had started a tradition of bullying the Turks, now Turkey's longtime nemesis was ready for a new chapter of cooperation—under Putin the Great.

Putin's outreach facilitated a power-sharing agreement in Syria that would soon be unveiled (as explained below). This meeting may have been when Putin convinced Erdogan to sell Turkey a Russian-made S-400 missile-defense system. The Russian president recognized that this was a small price for Erdogan to pay for Russian protection and good feeling. Simple though the move might have been, Putin, the master chess player, understood that he could achieve much strategically through such a tactical gesture. The sale initiated a deep and lasting rift between Washington and Ankara.

Erdogan's commitment to buy the Russian missile-defense system set Turkey on a collision course with the United States, resulting in U.S. sanctions against Ankara in 2019 and 2020, threatening to sever eight decades of bilateral defense-industrial ties. Putin is thus nearing a goal desired by successive Russian leaders since 1945–46, when Turkey picked the United States as its key global ally. Whether the current window of opportunity survives various Turkish-Russian tensions in Syria and Libya—and the possibility that President Joe Biden could "win" Erdogan back, given the extent to which the latter sees Putin as his protector—remains to be seen, of course.

The coup events, all told, suggested clearly to Erdogan who was on his side. At the time, among Turkey's key NATO allies, only Britain rushed to reach out, with Minister for Europe and the Americas Alan Duncan visiting Ankara on July 21.[25] The previous month, Britain's Brexit referendum promised to move London to the EU's periphery, leading it to seek global allies such as Turkey. Duncan's Ankara visit thus set up the UK as a rare NATO member with a direct line to Erdogan.

"Sharing" Syria

Following Putin's outreach, he and Erdogan spoke often, resulting in a series of ad hoc deals in Syria. The Russian leader has taken something from Erdogan in each call, often in return for efforts to undermine the U.S.-backed YPG. Specifically, on August 24, 2016, only six weeks after the coup and fifteen days after his meeting with Erdogan at Konstantinovsky, Putin gave his Turkish counterpart the green light to send troops into Syria. After some intense fighting against the Islamic State, Turkey seized from the jihadist group the Jarabulus pocket along the border, allowing Ankara to create a wedge against YPG-held territories in northern Syria.

The cost for Erdogan was accepting a Moscow- and Damascus-led assault on rebel-held east Aleppo. Turkish pressure on the rebels to abandon Aleppo city meant that Assad would soon take over remaining rebel-held parts of Syria's largest city, quashing Syrian opposition hopes of using it as a launchpad to take over the capital.[26] Coupled with the U.S. winding down of "Timber Sycamore," as the initiative to arm the Syrian rebels was known, the capitulation on Aleppo city relegated the armed opposition to perpetual defense on the peripheries of northern Syria. Only six weeks after the failed coup attempt, Putin had thus already "won" the war in Syria, ensuring that Ankara had all but lost its path to oust Assad.

Thereafter, in January 2018, with the goal of splitting Washington and Ankara further apart, Putin allowed Erdogan to operate his air force over the YPG's Afrin enclave in northwest Syria, then occupy it, in exchange for Erdogan's tacit approval for an Assad-regime assault on East Ghouta. His message to Erdogan and the Turkish public was clear: The United States works with your enemy, the YPG in Syria, while I am helping you tear it down. Who is your *real* friend?

The stage was just about set for Ankara's direct assault against the YPG in northeast Syria, where U.S.-YPG cooperation had been building since the Islamic State attack on Kobane in 2014. In October 2019, after a controversial partial U.S. troop withdrawal ordered by President Trump,[27] Turkish troops attacked YPG forces along Syria's border with Turkey. This move presented U.S. military personnel working with the Kurdish group with the choice to either withdraw or shoot at NATO-ally troops. They chose the former, relocating closer to Syria's border with Iraq and allowing Turkish troops to inflict a tactical defeat on the YPG.

The Turkish military was not alone in filling the vacuum left by withdrawing U.S. forces, though. Assad-regime and Russian troops occupied an extensive buffer zone of their own, along the contact lines between Turkish and Turkish-supported forces and the YPG. This has enabled Russian forces a growing role east of the Euphrates—including joint patrolling with Turkish forces in some areas and with YPG forces in others—as well as assistance to Assad's military footprint in northeast Syria. Putin has in this way secured the U.S. pullback from large parts of northeast Syria without firing a bullet.

Notes

1	See, e.g., Soner Cagaptay, "UN Plan Fails in Cyprus: Implications for Turkey, the European Union, and the United States," PolicyWatch 865, Washington Institute for Near East Policy, April 29, 2004, https://www.washingtoninstitute.org/policy-analysis/un-plan-fails-cyprus-implications-turkey-european-union-and-united-states.

2	Soner Cagaptay, *Erdogan's Empire: Turkey and the Politics of the Middle East* (London: I.B. Tauris, 2019).

3	Kemal Kirisci and Basak Yavcan, "As COVID-19 Worsens Precarity for Refugees, Turkey and the EU Must Work Together," Brookings Institution, June 11, 2020, https://www.brookings.edu/blog/order-from-chaos/2020/06/11/as-covid-19-worsens-precarity-for-refugees-turkey-and-the-eu-must-work-together/.

4	Cagaptay, *Erdogan's Empire*, 41–61.

5	Bianet, News List Archives, https://bianet.org/english/politics/176388-erdogan-changes-opinion-on-mavi-marmara-crisis.

6	Soner Cagaptay, *The Rise of Turkey* (Potomac, 2014), 151.

7	Ibid., 138.

8	Author in conversation with a friend.

9 Ibid., 32.

10 "The Rise of Political Islam and the AKP," Hoover Institution.

11 See "The Syrian Disaster" in Cagaptay, *Erdogan's Empire*.

12 Cagaptay, *Erdogan's Empire*, 110.

13 "Is Turkey Turning Its Back on the West?" *Economist*, October 21, 2010, https://www.economist.com/leaders/2010/10/21/is-turkey-turning-its-back-on-the-west.

14 "Timeline: The Rise, Spread, and Fall of the Islamic State," Wilson Center, October 28, 2019, https://www.wilsoncenter.org/article/timeline-the-rise-spread-and-fall-the-islamic-state.

15 Aaron Stein, "Reconciling U.S.-Turkish Interests in Northern Syria," discussion paper, Council on Foreign Relations, February 2017, https://www.cfr.org/sites/default/files/pdf/2017/02/Discussion_Paper_Stein_Syria_Turkey_OR.pdf.

16 Reilly Barry, "Erdogan the Good or Erdogan the Bad? A Conversation with Soner Cagaptay on U.S.-Turkey Relations Following U.S. Withdrawal from Syria," Harvard Kennedy School, October 25, 2019, https://jmepp.hkspublications.org/2019/10/25/erdogan-turkey-us-relations-syria/; "All Who Associate with PKK Are Legitimate Targets, Turkish FM Says," *Ahval*, June 19, 2020, https://ahvalnews.com/northern-syria/all-who-associate-pkk-are-legitimate-targets-turkish-fm-says.

17 Paul Sonne and Emre Peker, "Russia's Vladimir Putin Places Sanctions Against Ankara over Downing of Fighter Plane," *Wall Street Journal*, November 29, 2015, https://www.wsj.com/articles/russian-president-vladimir-putin-calls-for-sanctions-against-turkey-1448736083.

18 "Foreign Trade Statistics," Turkish Statistical Institute, August 2018.

19 Senior Turkish official, correspondence with author, April 12, 2016.

20 European and U.S. officials, correspondence with author, July 18 and 19, 2016, respectively.

21 Jared Malsin, "After Failed Coup a Vengeful Recep Tayyip Erdogan Has Turkey's Future in His Hands," *Time*, July 18, 2016," https://time.com/4410962/after-failed-coup-a-vengeful-recep-tayyip-erdogan-has-turkeys-future-in-his-hands/.

22 "Turkey Timeline: Here's How the Coup Attempt Unfolded," Al Jazeera, July 16, 2016, https://www.aljazeera.com/news/2016/7/16/turkey-timeline-heres-how-the-coup-attempt-unfolded.

23 "Bekir Bozdag: ABD Darbe Girisimini Gulen'in Yaptigini Cok iyi Biliyor," *Haberturk*, July 24, 2016, https://www.haberturk.com/dunya/haber/1271081-bekir-bozdag-abd-darbe-girisimini-gulenin-yaptigini-cok-iyi-biliyor.

24 Asli Aydintasbas, "Unhappy Anniversary: Turkey's Failed Coup and the S-400," European Council on Foreign Relations, July 17, 2019, https://www.ecfr.eu/article/commentary_unhappy_anniversary_turkeys_failed_coup_and_the_s_400.

25 Turkish Ministry of Foreign Affairs, "Disisleri Bakani Sayin Cavusoglu'nun Ingiltere Disisleri Bakanligi'nda Avrupa ve Amerika'dan Sorumlu Devlet Bakani Allen Duncan'i Kabulu Hakkinda Arka Plan Notu," n.d., http://www.mfa.gov.tr/disisleri-bakani-sayin-cavusoglu_nun-ingiltere-disisleri-bakanligi_nda--avrupa-ve-amerika_dan-sorumlu--devlet-bakani-allen-dunca.tr.mfa.

26 See "Building Soft Power," in Cagaptay, *Erdogan's Empire*.

27 Julian E. Barnes and Eric Schmitt, "Trump Orders Withdrawal of U.S. Troops from Northern Syria," *New York Times*, October 13, 2019, https://www.nytimes.com/2019/10/13/us/politics/mark-esper-syria-kurds-turkey.html.

7

Between Putin and Biden

Turkey's relations with Russia are historically more fraught than those with the United States, but both dynamics experience their particular strains. Still, the question of whether Erdogan and Putin can be counted as allies deserves special attention.

Are Turkey and Russia Allies?

While the Erdogan-Putin relationship is currently strong—the Turkish president considers his Russian counterpart his protector and dealmaking partner—the same cannot be said for Turkish-Russian ties. Namely, Ankara and Moscow disagree regarding Russia's annexation of Crimea—where Turkey is cooperating with Ukraine against Russia—the Cyprus conflict, and the eastern Mediterranean strategic environment, where Russia's traditional ally is Greece. The ceasefire between Turkish- and Russian-backed forces in Libya is tenuous as of early 2021 and not yet supported by a power-sharing deal, as exists in Syria. What is more, it is not at all certain that Putin—who brokered a ceasefire between Turkey's ally Azerbaijan and his own ally Armenia in the disputed Nagorno-Karabakh region—will actually establish the trade corridor envisioned in his November 2020 peace deal; the corridor would run from the Azerbaijani exclave of Nakhichevan, which borders Turkey, via Armenia into Azerbaijan proper. For all practical purposes, therefore, the Turkish-Russian relationship is not based on a shared strategic vision but rather on situational and fluid partnering, although it should be added that Erdogan and Putin both relish challenging the U.S.-led international order.

Ankara, Moscow, and the PKK

In addition, Ankara has incurred significant risk in Syria, despite temporarily managing to push the YPG away from the Turkish border, once again driven by Moscow. Future challenges for Erdogan include the possibility that Putin will place serious pressure on Turkey to vacate the Syrian territory it now occupies. Equally possible is that the PKK-aligned YPG will ultimately cut a deal with Moscow and the Syrian regime to fight against Turkey and its proxies. The Turks cannot trust the Russians to deliver a quiet or secure border with Syria, and will probably face the long-term prospect of insurgency and terrorism there or at the point of contact between their forces and proxies and the YPG or Assad's fighters.

Furthermore, Turkey will eventually face a renewed Assad-PKK alliance, probably with Russia's tacit blessing. The relationship between the Assad regime and the PKK is nearly as old as the regime itself. Damascus has hosted the PKK for decades and has allowed it to use Syrian territory as a base from which to carry out attacks into Turkey. Even today, YPG and regime forces cooperatively oppose Turkish and Turkish-supported forces in several areas in Syria: e.g., Tal Rifaat, Manbij, and Tal Tamer.

Only in October 1998 did the Assad regime "ban" the PKK—and then only when Ankara threatened to invade unless Damascus stopped harboring the group. In 2006, on a visit to Syria, though, I saw numerous PKK banners and posters across towns and villages in the north, despite the group being apparently illegal. This seriously called into question what being outlawed meant, especially in a police state like Syria.[1] Now, should Erdogan eventually agree to live with Assad, the regime could similarly sweep the YPG under the rug without actually shutting it down. The Syrian leader surely will not forget that Erdogan sought to have him ousted, and he may well want to preserve the YPG's capabilities for a rainy day.

Moscow, too, has PKK ties as old as the Cold War, and most of the group's leaders—many of whom joined in the 1970s—have a pro-Soviet pedigree. Whatever he promises Erdogan, Putin is unlikely to insist that Assad completely suppress the PKK in Syria. Ultimately, Russia's historical relationship with the PKK will serve as a key lever should the Turkish leader deviate from Moscow in international affairs. Libya is a case in point.

The Balance in Libya

As in Syria, Putin has used Libya's civil war to create a strategic vulnerability for Ankara—playing both arsonist and firefighter, and once again taking advantage of the presence of multiple on-the-ground actors opposing Ankara.

When the North African country descended into civil war in 2014, Erdogan threw his support behind the mainly political Islamist factions in Tripoli's Western-based Operation Dawn coalition, which opposed Operation Dignity, led by Khalifa Haftar in Tobruk in the east. The Tripoli-based coalition evolved after 2015 into the Government of National Accord (GNA), recognized by the United Nations as the legitimate interim government but increasingly opposed by the Tobruk-based Libyan National Army (LNA) that evolved from Operation Dignity.

Egyptian president Abdul Fattah al-Sisi and his ally the United Arab Emirates, worried about the ascent of political Islam in nearby Libya—and eager to undermine Erdogan—were quick to assist Haftar's forces and carried out airstrikes targeting the Tripoli factions. By 2019, these strikes broadened into a general offensive against the GNA, and a siege of the capital, Tripoli; Haftar-aligned forces have been credibly accused of mass killings in Tarhuna and elsewhere during the siege. Turkey sought to counter these moves by providing the GNA with drones of its own, as well as additional weapons and armored personnel carriers.

Ankara's Libya policy has multiple drivers. First, Turkey wants to collect on Qadhafi-era debt—totaling billions of dollars—and also to have access to new and lucrative construction contracts in the war-torn but oil-rich country. The historical record indicates strongly that Turks are builders as a nation—for instance, the Ottoman cultural legacy, as widely known, includes few scientific inventions or plays, but dozens, if not hundreds, of magnificently constructed bridges, mosques, palaces, and *imarets* (soup kitchens). Contemporary trends, meanwhile, suggest that construction is what Turks do best in international business, and this is also the case regarding Libya.

Second, in Libya, Erdogan wants to humiliate Egypt's President Sisi, the eastern Mediterranean leader with whom Turkey's president is least likely to reconcile—with Syria's Assad and Israel's Binyamin Netanyahu next in line.[2] There's a mirror-image component to Erdogan's dynamic with Sisi: Erdogan is the political Islamist who has locked up secularist generals, and Sisi is the secularist general who has locked up political Islamists. Erdogan would like nothing more than to embarrass Sisi in Libya by defeating Haftar, and Sisi equally would relish embarrassing Erdogan by helping Haftar take Tripoli.

What is more in Libya, this time joined by Turkey's military and Foreign Ministry, Erdogan wants to undermine Ankara's other Middle East nemesis, the UAE, which also supports Haftar. But there is more to the UAE angle as seen from Turkey. Ankara officials feel that Abu Dhabi is turning up behind every anti-Turkish initiative these days—from support to publications critical of Turkey to the Syrian crisis, where the UAE has allegedly offered cash to the Assad regime, encouraging it to attack Turkish troops.[3]

Another driver of Turkey's Libya policy is its sense of isolation in the eastern Mediterranean, a sentiment that has gradually darkened since the rupture of Turkish-Israeli ties in 2010 and Erdogan's regional policy miscalculations during the Arab uprisings. Across the region, Turkey has found itself pitted against an emerging coalition of old and new adversaries, mainly Cyprus, Egypt, Greece, and Israel. Given its cool-to-hostile relations with these states, Ankara is alarmed by the rate at which they have come together in strategic cooperation, including joint diplomatic, energy, and military initiatives.

Soon after coming to power in June 2014, for example, Sisi opened talks with Greece to delineate their maritime economic areas. He then held a three-way summit in November 2014 to promote a deal for supplying natural gas to Egypt from undersea fields off the coast of Cyprus. Cairo also hosted the inaugural meeting of the East Mediterranean Gas Forum in January 2019, notably excluding Turkey.

In November 2019, Ankara forged a new maritime agreement with Tripoli in part to counter such cooperation. The accord established a virtual maritime axis between Dalaman on Turkey's southwest coast and Darnah on Libya's northeast coast (far from the GNA's practical area of control). In Erdogan's view, drawing this line allowed him to cut into the emerging Cyprus-Egypt-Greece-Israel maritime bloc, while simultaneously pushing back against Egypt and the UAE's pressure on the GNA.[4]

The Greek angle in this dynamic is especially important in getting Turkey roused about Libya. There was a time, in the later twentieth century, when Greece was a power comparable to Turkey, including the size of its economy and military. No longer. Today, Turkey's economy is nearly three times that of Greece. In numeric terms, Turkey's army and general population surpass those of Greece. Turkish elites remain as worried about "Greek maritime power," especially Greece's presence in the seas surrounding Turkey, as Greek elites are about "Turkish power" in general.[5]

Greece and Turkey share a near obsession with each other politically, an attitude rooted in relations during the foundational years of the two modern states. In something of a twist, Greece liberated itself from Turkish occupation in the 1820s and Turkey liberated itself from Greek occupation in the 1920s. During these two ruptures, Greek and Turkish populations who had lived together for nearly a thousand years—since the arrival of Seljuk Turks in the Anatolian peninsula in the 1070s—violently came apart, moving into their respective "separate homes." Yet the bloody unraveling has produced the mutual political fixation, which perhaps can be likened to the current state of India-Pakistan relations shaped by the 1947 partition. With Turkey's economic and demographic growth now outpacing that of Greece, Athens is undoubtedly the more worried of the two capitals. But Turkish insecurities remain acute in the maritime sphere, where there is a fear of being boxed in. Accordingly, in Libya, Greek elites are worried about rising Turkish power, while Ankara is similarly concerned that if the anti-Turkey Haftar triumphs, Greece will use him to block Turkish aspirations in the eastern Mediterranean.

Whatever role President Biden decides to play in arbitrating Turkish-Greek tensions in the eastern Mediterranean, Athens is likely to emerge as the winner, considering the traditional political balance among Greece, Turkey, and the United States. Since the beginning of the Cold War, Washington has viewed Turkey as the linchpin of its eastern Mediterranean security architecture, along with Israel. Thanks to the legacy of the Erdogan era, though, this policy is now shifting, and Washington has begun regarding Greece as the more reliable ally, replacing Turkey. This shift is indeed happening slowly—

akin to a tanker altering course on open seas—but it has long-term ramifications for U.S.-Turkish ties: Washington is signaling to Ankara that Greece has become the "new Turkey."

From the French angle, too, developments in recent years have frayed ties between the two NATO allies to such an extent that this time they have become hostile. In Libya specifically, Paris is competing with Ankara for the same postwar contracts. Paris also militarily backs the UAE, its closest ally in the Arab Middle East, against Turkey in Libya (see chapter 10 for further discussion of French-Turkish tensions).

Related is the return of Great Power competition to the Mediterranean. Paris, which has viewed the sea's southern basin, especially along the Maghreb, as its sphere of influence since it wrested Algeria from the Ottomans in 1830, has taken note of Turkey's forays into this area, as well as Erdogan's frequent rhetoric targeting former French president Nicolas Sarkozy.[6] This helps explain France's alliance with Turkish opponents such as the UAE, as well as Greece and Egypt.

Moreover, unlike other NATO members in Europe, such as Germany, which is exposed to Turkish politics through a large Turkish diaspora population domestically and deep bilateral economic and social ties, France does not feel as exposed to Turkey and, therefore, is not interested in placating Ankara. These factors have led Paris to become a member of the anti-GNA alliance in Libya and the anti-Turkish alignment in the eastern Mediterranean in general. Such developments have made the GNA increasingly dependent on Ankara for military reasons: namely, a lack of other allies willing to provide arms capable of countering Haftar's Libyan National Army drones—supplied by the UAE—and the French and Egyptian military support Haftar enjoys.

In early 2019, thanks to increasing Turkish support to the GNA, the war in Libya appeared headed toward some sort of stasis—that is, until Putin entered the theater that summer. The introduction of Russian support to Haftar in the form of mercenaries, under the Wagner Group, added new technology and precision to the general's war against Tripoli, suddenly making him a mortal threat to the GNA. Then, in December 2019, Libya's capital almost came within Haftar's grasp. Realizing that his core interests in Libya were under threat— that if Haftar captured Tripoli, he would rip up Libya's maritime treaty with Ankara, and demand that Erdogan forget about Qadhafi-era debt or new contracts—Erdogan rushed to Moscow for a ceasefire deal.

Arsonist-turned-firefighter Putin hosted a "peace conference" in Moscow on January 13, 2020. Unsurprisingly, the conference failed to produce a lasting ceasefire, and Putin—who excels in linking conflicts and making the countries involved dependent on him for their resolution—had just made his indelible point to Erdogan: if he rejected Putin's "offers" in Syria, or canceled the S-400 sale, things could get much worse for Ankara in Libya.

In early 2020, Erdogan dramatically ramped up the quantity and quality of its military support to the GNA. A counteroffensive by GNA-aligned forces—backed by Turkish drones and commandos, supplied through a major air- and sealift, and bolstered by Syrian militiamen brought in by Turkey—pushed LNA forces out of most of western Libya, back to the Sirte–al-Jufra line. Turkey also succeeded in establishing a major air base at al-Watiyah in western Libya, as well as training bases and port facilities on the coast. Turkish support helped the Tripoli government fend off Haftar's advances, but Erdogan remains sensitive to Putin's demands in Libya. Absent a robust U.S. military role in the country, an unlikely scenario under President Biden,[7] the future promises a new status quo in which Ankara and Moscow are key power-sharing entities. Thus, Putin and Erdogan find themselves tangled in two different civil wars.

The South Caucasus "Deal"

Similarly, Erdogan and Putin have recently entered into a tenuous influence-sharing agreement in the South Caucasus, where Azeri-Armenian tensions flared in July 2020 over the Armenian-occupied Azeri region of Nagorno-Karabakh. Turkey, which previously backed Azerbaijan politically against Armenia, now provided military assistance in the form of drones and other military hardware, tipping the balance of power on the ground further in Baku's favor.[8] This allowed Azerbaijan to swiftly push back against Armenian forces, and when it looked as if Stepanakert—the Nagorno-Karabakh capital—was in the Azeris' reach, Putin interfered by presenting a "peace plan."

The plan required Armenia to withdraw its forces from Nagorno-Karabakh but also interjects Russia as a peacekeeper into the broader area, within Azerbaijan. The somewhat opaque plan provides an uncertain role for Turkey in maintaining peace, and a yet-to-be determined land and trade corridor (noted earlier) connecting the Azeri enclave of Nakhichevan, bordering Turkey, to Azerbaijan proper via Armenia. This arrangement positions Putin as not only Erdogan's partner in the South Caucasus, in yet another feeble power-sharing agreement, but also a kingmaker in another conflict involving Turkey.

Playing with Putin

In the asymmetrical Russian-Turkish relationship, Putin has economic and military advantages, but has had to deal with Erdogan's greater initiative and commitment on specific issues in areas geographically proximate to Turkey. Ankara's leverage in Syria stems from Putin's desire to end the war there on his own political track, the so-called Astana process, for which he needs Turkish participation to have international legitimacy. If Turkey left the Astana process, whose third member is Iran, it would simply look like a "friends of Assad" club, without any potentially dissenting member. Turkey is also willing to incur greater military costs to maintain its position in Syria than Russia is willing to incur to oust them.

Idlib, the last Syrian province where anti-Assad rebels are still standing, is a case in point.[9] In a difficult balancing act for Putin, he must keep both Erdogan and Assad happy. A test occurred in December 2019, when Assad violated an existing ceasefire and Putin followed suit to support his ally. Hostilities resulted in the killing of thirty-three Turkish troops in February 2020, caused by suspected Assad-regime airstrikes in which Russian planes accompanied Syrian planes.[10] This was the highest single-day casualty count for the Turkish military since Ankara got involved in the Syrian war in 2012, and perhaps Putin's gravest error regarding Turkey in Syria to date.

Erdogan responded to save face domestically, saying that Turkey would hit Syrian forces "anywhere" if one more Turkish soldier was hurt,[11] and Putin understood this necessity. Meanwhile, the United States, in pronouncing its support for the Turkish position in Idlib, wisely took advantage of the window to demonstrate to Erdogan that he would be stronger against Russia with U.S. backing.[12] In turn, this U.S. support nudged Putin to allow the Turkish military to pummel Assad-regime forces in Idlib through a well-executed campaign involving drones, standoff air munitions, and long-range artillery.[13] This permission comports with Putin's long-game strategy in Syria, based on the principle of never entirely alienating Turkey. The Russian leader can thus keep Ankara as close to Moscow as possible, and simultaneously as far away from NATO as possible.

Taking the longer historical view, Putin knows that tightening the screws too much could push Turkey back toward NATO—a repeat of Stalin's misstep in the 1945–46 period when the Soviet dictator threatened Turkey, demanding territory from Ankara. But, it is worth clarifying, Russia's leader does not necessarily want to see Turkey leave NATO but rather remain in the alliance as a disgruntled member, thereby diluting its effectiveness. Is it possible Putin already has Turkey and Erdogan where he wants them?

After nearly destroying Assad's military, Erdogan stopped short of moving further against him, or threatening Damascus, most probably because he often heeds Putin's warnings. Although Turkey had successfully humiliated Assad-regime forces in Idlib, at the peace table with Putin, Erdogan ended up conceding nearly one-third of the province's territory to Assad. Just as Putin does not want a rupture with Erdogan, Erdogan does not want a rupture with Putin. Both leaders had reason enough to produce a new Idlib deal in March 2020, signed in Moscow.[14]

The Turkish president has relied on his Russian counterpart diplomatically since Putin reached out to him following the failed 2016 coup attempt, and Erdogan's frayed international relationships have only deepened his dependence on this support since then. Moreover, Russia's military capabilities and historical scorecard against Turkey make Erdogan wary of a major conflict. Finally, since their August 2016 meeting at the Konstantinovsky Palace, Erdogan appears to have valued Putin as his protector. After all, Putin has established his credentials as the protector of other, even more threatened leaders globally, from Assad in Damascus to Venezuelan leader Nicolas Maduro in Caracas.

Menacing Persians

Whereas Erdogan and Putin ultimately have been striving to get along, Iran often plays the spoiler in this relationship, as it did in January 2020, when Tehran-backed militias joined Assad's forces in attacking Turkish troops in Idlib.[15] As a general matter, Iran wants

Turkey to recognize Syria as part of Tehran's sphere of influence.

Historically speaking, the Ottoman and Safavid Empires became neighbors in the fifteenth century, at which point they started challenging each other for control of territories along their shared borderlands. After fighting a series of debilitating wars spanning 1473–1639 that eventually bankrupted their treasuries—a seventeenth-century race to the bottom—the Turks and Persians settled on terms for power parity, agreeing to avoid future conflict at any cost. Remarkably, the section of Ottoman-Safavid border drawn up in 1639 remains mostly intact today, making it the longest-standing frontier in the Middle East. Viewing each other through the prism of power parity and as historical rivals, Turkey and Iran have thus avoided fighting except in cases where one perceived the other to be weak or vulnerable. This tradition continued through the collapse of the Ottoman Empire and into the twentieth century.[16]

But the Syrian conflict has tested the two nations' historical power parity, with Tehran viewing Ankara's support to rebels fighting the Iran-backed regime as a violation of the arrangement, and the Turks equally concerned over growing Iranian domination of the Syrian state. At this stage, Tehran, whose fortunes and allies have been ascendant in Syria over the past decade, will attempt to cement its current relative advantage and reset the historic power parity with Ankara on its own terms. From Iran's perspective, this would necessitate a complete cessation of Turkish support to anti-Assad rebels. In this context, every step Iran takes in Syria with respect to Turkey—including, e.g., regarding Erdogan-Putin deals in Idlib—serves the broader Iranian goal of locking in a new balance of power in Syria and the Levant, wherein Turkey recognizes Iranian control over Syria. Accordingly, Tehran is likely to play bad cop to Moscow's good cop vis-à-vis Erdogan in Syria, complicating matters for the Turkish president. This was most recently the case during the December 2019 Idlib crisis and in February–March 2020, when Iran-backed

Hezbollah fighters joined the fighting against Turkey with Assad's troops while Erdogan and Putin were negotiating a way to diffuse the conflict.[17] Turkey is not likely to acquiesce to Iranian dominance, especially near the Turkish-Syrian border, nor to abandon its Syrian proxies (or invite them to migrate to Turkey).

Idlib and Refugees

The current dynamic in Syria begs the question of how Erdogan, Putin, Assad, and Iranian president Hassan Rouhani (or his successor in 2021) will thread the needle regarding the final status of Syria's Idlib province and, more specifically, its civilian population of over two million. As of early 2021, Turkish-backed rebels still hold more than a third of Idlib's territory, but Tehran supports Assad's goal of recapturing these areas. Putin almost certainly has the tools to enforce a power-sharing deal that would grant Assad more territory, but past such arrangements have driven civilians—fearing persecution at the Syrian regime's hands—into the Turkish-controlled zone.

The Syrian refugee situation in Turkey bears elaborating here. Since 2012, nearly four million Syrians have fled their country for neighboring Turkey. As of 2020, Syrians constituted a nearly 5 percent addition to Turkey's population of some 84 million—which, in the U.S. context, would equal nearly 16 million refugees over less than a decade, and in Britain, more than 3 million refugees over the same span. Turkey's government and people deserve praise for the welcome they have extended to the refugees, which helped prevent a humanitarian disaster, despite the huge demographic and social burdens they have presented.[18] Beginning in 2018, however, the Turkish economic slowdown has increased anti-refugee sentiment, and a further influx from Idlib could create unsustainable political headwinds for Erdogan.

Managing President Biden

The state of the Turkish economy will force Erdogan to make adjustments, including likely pivoting a bit toward the United States. Washington holds the "golden vote" at the International Monetary Fund, and is the only financial power, other than China, that could bail Turkey out if its economy experienced a meltdown. China will resist coming to Turkey's aid, largely because of the Uyghur angle. China considers the Uyghurs, Muslim residents of China's Xinjiang region, to be a threat to the country's soft underbelly, and a significant Uyghur diaspora is based in Turkey.[19] For his own part, Erdogan is trying to balance Turkey's need for Chinese investment with the realities of the country's self-described representation of the world's oppressed Muslims and Turks. Perhaps unsurprisingly, Erdogan has been personally quiet on the Uyghur issue for nearly a decade.

In a large sense, Erdogan appreciates Washington's financial role globally and has recently tempered his critiques of the White House in the interest of shielding Turkey's economy from global financial shocks, an approach that also protects his own standing. As a rule of thumb, Turkey's economy does better when Ankara has good ties with Washington and it suffers amid strained U.S. ties.[20]

Erdogan has masterfully played a succession of U.S. presidents, even at times winning their hearts. To George W. Bush, Erdogan presented himself as a faithful Muslim with whom Bush, himself a faithful Christian, could work. To Barack Obama, Erdogan proffered himself as a "window to the Muslim world." And most recently, to Donald Trump, Erdogan cast himself as a partner for "making deals." Now, with Biden, Erdogan will become the "internationalist, reformer, and healer" president. But Biden knows Erdogan, has dealt with him for more than a decade, and is not naive to his ways and means. "Winning" Biden's heart will be Erdogan's toughest challenge to date with any U.S. president.

Keeping Both Moscow and Washington Happy

On the strategic side, given U.S. support in Idlib, Erdogan has rediscovered an appreciation for Washington.[21] The Biden administration will take advantage of this, likely upholding a longstanding executive branch preference to do all it can to keep Turkey on its side. Yet even if the new U.S. administration—and its successors—does not give up on Turkey, Washington should be realistic regarding its expectations of Erdogan. It is unlikely, for instance, that he will cancel the S-400 deal with Russia, since he has decided to also cultivate good ties with Putin. This is the case despite the sanctions imposed by the Trump administration in its closing months.[22]

Given his competing needs, Erdogan will keep playing Russia and the United States against each other, while staying engaged in various wars. Yet a Turkish economic implosion could strain the Erdogan-Putin relationship—pushing the Turkish leader toward Washington—and also force Ankara to scale down its involvement in Syria and Libya. Recent fighting between Turkish and Syrian-regime forces in Idlib "has reminded Erdogan that with or without a deal, he cannot stand up to Russia alone, and that he is better off repairing his ties with Washington."[23] But it may not be so easy for Erdogan to win Biden's heart—not only because the U.S. president has dealt with Erdogan the "shape-shifter" before and is, therefore, unlikely to fall for him, but also because Erdogan's domestic crackdown will make it just about impossible for Biden to fully embrace him.

Notes

1 "Statement Made by Ismail Cem, Foreign Minister, on the Special
   Security Meeting Held Between Turkey and Syria, October 20, 1998
   (Unofficial Translation)," Ministry of Foreign Affairs, October 20, 1998,
   available at https://web.archive.org/web/20160301105039/http://www.
   mfa.gov.tr/_p_statement-made-by-ismail-cem_-foreign-minister_-
   on-the-special-security-meeting-held-between-turkey-and-syria_br_
   october-20_-1998_br__unofficial-translation___p_.en.mfa.

2 "Netanyahu Hits Back at 'Turkey's Dictator Erdogan,'" France 24, March
   13, 2019, https://www.france24.com/en/20190313-netanyahu-hits-back-
   turkeys-dictator-erdogan; Associated Press, "Turkish, Israeli Name
   Calling Covers 'Tyrant' to 'Dictator,'" March 13, 2019, https://apnews.
   com/article/2b181366a2204e2f88547c9f747a8997.

3 Cengiz Candar, "Turkey-UAE Rift May Have Unintended Spillover,"
   Al-Monitor, December 22, 2017, https://www.al-monitor.com/pulse/
   originals/2017/12/turkey-uae-conflict-may-spillover-into-gulf.html;
   "UAE Pushed Assad Regime to Break Idlib Cease-Fire, Report Claims,"
   Daily Sabah, April 8, 2020, https://www.dailysabah.com/world/syrian-
   crisis/uae-pushed-assad-regime-to-break-idlib-cease-fire-report-claims.

4 Soner Cagaptay, "This map explains all you need know to answer
   how serious Turkey is regarding its support to Tripoli in Libya's civil
   war. Contact with Libyan sea space allows Ankara to cut into Israeli-
   Egyptian-Cypriot-Greek axis boxing Turkey in eastern Mediterranean,"
   post on Twitter, December 30, 2019, 10:46 a.m., https://twitter.com/
   SonerCagaptay/status/1211674883853291521.

5 Turkish official Cagatay Erciyes tweeted on this topic, on October 12,
   2020, but his post has since been blocked: https://twitter.com/CErciyes/
   status/131565080881448960.

6 "Be Man of Your Word, Erdogan Tells Sarkozy," *Hurriyet Daily News*,
   December 17, 2011, https://www.hurriyetdailynews.com/be-man-of-
   your-word-erdogan-tells-sarkozy-9406.

7 Jason Pack and Wolfgang Pusztai, *Turning the Tide: How Turkey Won the War for Tripoli* (Middle East Institute, 2020), https://www.mei.edu/publications/turning-tide-how-turkey-won-war-tripoli.

8 Dorian Jones, "Turkish Drone Power Displayed in Nagorno-Karabakh Conflict," Voice of America, October 13, 2020, https://www.voanews.com/middle-east/turkish-drone-power-displayed-nagorno-karabakh-conflict.

9 Aymenn Jawad al-Tamimi, *Idlib and Its Environs: Narrowing Prospects for a Rebel Holdout* (Washington DC: Washington Institute, 2020), https://www.washingtoninstitute.org/policy-analysis/idlib-and-its-environs-narrowing-prospects-rebel-holdout.

10 Bethan McKernan, "Dozens of Turkish Soldiers Killed in Strike in Idlib in Syria," *Guardian*, February 28, 2020, https://www.theguardian.com/world/2020/feb/27/dozens-of-turkish-soldiers-killed-in-strike-in-idlib-in-syria-reports-say.

11 "Erdogan: Turkey Will Hit Syrian Government Forces 'Anywhere,'" Al Jazeera, February 12, 2020, https://www.aljazeera.com/news/2020/2/12/erdogan-turkey-will-hit-syrian-government-forces-anywhere.

12 Sarah Dadouch, "U.S. Officials Visit Turkey's Border with Syria, Emphasize Support for NATO Ally," *Washington Post*, March 3, 2020, https://www.washingtonpost.com/world/middle_east/us-officials-visit-turkeys-border-with-syria-emphasize-support-for-nato-ally/2020/03/03/7bfce6c2-5d58-11ea-ac50-18701e14e06d_story.html.

13 "Syria War: Turkey Intensifies Idlib Onslaught After Air Strike," BBC News, March 1, 2020, https://www.bbc.com/news/world-middle-east-51697980.

14 "Syria War: Russia and Turkey Agree [*sic*] Idlib Ceasefire," BBC, March 5, 2020, https://www.bbc.com/news/world-middle-east-51747592.

15 Hamidreza Azizi, "What Brought Iranian Forces to Idlib Front?" Al-Monitor, February 5, 2020, https://www.al-monitor.com/pulse/originals/2020/02/iran-battlefield-idlib-syria-soleimani.html.

16 Soner Cagaptay "Competing Persians," in *Erdogan's Empire: Turkey and the Politics of the Middle East* (London: I.B. Tauris, 2019).

17 Sena Guler, "Syria: Turkish Operations Spook Hezbollah Militias," Anadolu Agency, February 29, 2020, https://www.aa.com.tr/en/middle-east/syria-turkish-operations-spook-hezbollah-militias/1749773.

18 Soner Cagaptay and Deniz Yuksel, "Growing Anti-Syrian Sentiment in Turkey," PolicyWatch 3159, Washington Institute for the Near East Policy, August 5, 2019, https://www.washingtoninstitute.org/policy-analysis/view/growing-anti-syrian-sentiment-in-turkey.

19 Helen Davidson and Bethan McKernan, "Pressure on Turkey to Protect Uighurs as China Ratifies Extradition Treaty," *Guardian*, December 29, 2020, https://www.theguardian.com/world/2020/dec/29/pressure-on-turkey-to-protect-uighurs-as-china-ratifies-extradition-treaty.

20 Soner Cagaptay, "Turkey's Reconfigured Ties with the 'Strategic West,'" PolicyWatch 3187, Washington Institute for Near East Policy, September 25, 2019, https://www.washingtoninstitute.org/policy-analysis/turkeys-reconfigured-ties-strategic-west.

21 Ibid.

22 Lara Jakes, "U.S. Imposes Sanctions on Turkey over 2017 Purchase of Russian Missile Defenses," *New York Times*, December 14, 2020, https://www.nytimes.com/2020/12/14/us/politics/trump-turkey-missile-defense-sanctions.html.

23 Soner Cagaptay, "A New Erdogan-Putin Deal in Idlib May Help—for Now," PolicyWatch 3275, Washington Institute for Near East Policy, March 4, 2020, https://www.washingtoninstitute.org/policy-analysis/new-erdogan-putin-deal-idlib-may-help-now.

8

Democratic Tsunami

The state of the Turkish economy, suffering from anemic growth as of 2020, could well shape the remainder of Erdogan's career. Continued bleak economic news could prompt his popularity to plunge further. Luckily for him, Turkey's next scheduled presidential vote is not until 2023—but unluckily, his palace advisors on domestic politics have not, of late, helped him stay ahead of trouble.

Covid and Palace Politics

The public perception of Erdogan's Covid-19 response was at first negative, then neutral, and finally almost abysmal. The initial critique compared Erdogan's response to the far superior, independent public health measures implemented by opposition mayors.[1] In successive cases, Erdogan's palace (known as *saray* in Turkish) first refused to adopt such measures, only to coopt them later on, establishing a pattern of tardiness. Specifically, regarding the fundraising campaigns launched by Istanbul mayor Ekrem Imamoglu and Ankara mayor Mansur Yavas on March 30, 2020, the Erdogan palace had first banned these campaigns only to introduce its own fundraising initiative later the same day.[2]

Although Erdogan's palace has tried to take the lead in combating Covid, public perceptions have plummeted since the distortion and cover-up of virus-related statistics came to light in late September 2020 and with the country moving in and out of lockdowns, especially extreme and austere in Istanbul and not much different from the noncohesive policies enacted by various U.S. states.[3]

Moreover, while news stories have emerged suggesting Ankara has manipulated numbers regarding infections, Turkey's well-functioning healthcare system, a gift bestowed by Erdogan, has mostly helped the country's citizens weather the pandemic. In the end, however, his performance has been most damaging to himself. His initially slow response, along with the lack of a national plan, reinforced the public's establishment fatigue, creating an opportunity for the opposition leadership to govern effectively and outshine him.

Erdogan is an astute politician who has consolidated so much power that one can reasonably call him the quasi-sultan of Turkey's second republic. So why did this leader, at the peak of his power, falter in responding to Covid, and why did his administration betray such confusion in its steps? One answer could lie in Erdogan's very decision to change the country's political system from a parliamentary democracy into an executive-style presidency. This new system, approved narrowly in an April 2017 referendum, went into effect in July 2018. While consolidating power in Erdogan's hands, the system has also resulted in a hypercentralization of decisionmaking in Ankara—confined to a small group of advisors.[4]

Before 2018, Erdogan could draw on a large cadre of advisors, ministers, and government agencies to help him make sound decisions that resulted in election wins and competent decisionmaking during difficult times. Now, however, the president's small group of aides, with some notable exceptions, represents a downgrade from Turkey's historically competent institutions and their area-specific experts. Erdogan's erstwhile network of political confidants, which helped him win nearly a dozen elections, has also been sidelined in favor of a small inner circle.

Decades ago, diplomat Dennis Ross, then a young State Department official, published the trailblazing paper "Coalition Maintenance in the Soviet Union," in which he argued that within the Kremlin's confines, decisionmaking had become distorted.[5] Decisions were made, he explained, based not on the country's or party's best interests, but on what would best serve the narrow interests of one clique versus another. This distortion faithfully reflects the problem Erdogan and Turkey have frequently faced since the move to a presidential system, with political power now being centralized in the Ankara *saray*.

For instance, Erdogan's annulment of the March 2019 Istanbul municipal elections after Imamoglu's slim victory proved to be a grave error, indicative of the failure of palace politics. In this case, Erdogan's advisors, led by his son-in-law and Turkey's former finance minister Berat Albayrak, led a campaign to convince him to redo the Istanbul vote.[6] Even with all the state's resources mobilized against him, Imamoglu won the June 2019 contest by a landslide 800,000-vote margin, badly embarrassing the president.[7]

Albayrak's dismissal warrants a bit more attention. In fact, Erdogan showed his brutal pragmatism by sultanically accepting his own son-in-law's resignation as finance minister. Some suggested that Albayrak's resignation letter (see below), posted on Instagram on November 8, 2020, and laden with Islamic references, may have in fact reflected a social media hijacking by Erdogan. The language in the post included "May God help all of us see the end of all this," an unusual tone for a site usually populated by vacation pictures and social influencer exploits.[8] Years earlier, in May 2016, Erdogan had acted with similarly swift ruthlessness when he dismissed his foreign minister turned prime minister and longtime advisor Ahmet Davutoglu. This Machiavellian move toward Davutoglu had allowed Erdogan to recalibrate his Syria policy, dropping an erstwhile singular focus on targeting the Assad regime alone, and instead taking on the YPG, a move that received meticulous guidance from Putin in August the same year.

According to pro-Erdogan media, Albayrak had kept "secret" from his father-in-law the dismal condition of the national economy, including the treasury's depleted foreign exchange reserves—depleted in a vain attempt to prevent a drop in the value of the lira without raising interest rates.[9] Following Albayrak's ouster, the new Turkish finance minister, Lutfi Elvan, ended his predecessor's economic policies, deemed responsible for the country's low interest rates and low economic growth. After waiting three days to respond to Albayrak's departure, Erdogan issued a rather brusque and sultanly official statement accepting Albayrak's plea "to be excused of his duties."[10] Thus, the fall of Albayrak and Davutoglu before him suggests that even Erdogan's family members and closest advisors are there just to serve him, and that these officials are dispensable if the president's political survival calls for it. In other words, the *saray* exists thanks to Erdogan.

Democratic Resilience

A balance has emerged in Turkey wherein Erdogan has effectively emerged as the "new sultan" of the second republic but wherein democracy has shown signs of resiliency. One such instance was the Istanbul revote, whose outcome many analysts, myself included, failed to divine.[11]

Turkey became a multiparty democracy in 1950, and generations of its citizens have voted in free and fair elections. Turkey's citizens, who live in a country where their parents, grandparents, and in some cases even great-grandparents participated in free and fair elections, saw—as Erdogan did in June 2019—that leaders cannot easily rig the vote or win it through control of media and electoral bodies, absent support from a majority of the electorate. In old and established democracies, the electorate tends to have faith in the ballot box and to expect winners and losers alike to respect the outcome. Accordingly, in Turkey, opposition parties organized a masterful vote-protection campaign on June 23. Canan Kaftancioglu, the Istanbul head of the Republican People's Party (CHP), rallied nearly 100,000 volunteers to attend and document the ballot-tallying process, successfully preventing any attempts at fraud.[12] Many of her volunteers literally slept overnight on ballot bags to foil potential rigging. Together with other factors, Turkey's democratic legacy explains Imamoglu's landslide, with many Istanbullus changing their vote in June to send a clear message to Erdogan: *Respect the winner.*

Comparisons to the current Russian system, therefore, appear to be premature. What happened in Turkey in June 2019 could not happen in Russia—at least not under Putin—but *has* actually happened in authoritarian-trending states such as Hungary and Poland, where opposition mayoral candidates in Budapest and Warsaw triumphed, dealing a blow to their respective national and nativist populist leaders, Viktor Orban and Jaroslaw Kaczynski. So one might conclude that today's Turkey is neither a democracy nor a dictatorship but a "democracy run by an autocrat."

Given that Turkey led the way globally into populist authoritarianism, its relative democratic resilience and the opposition's success in Istanbul elections together might offer hints at the future for Hungary, Poland, Brazil, and other states that have entered the cycle.[13] Britain and the United States might be applicable cases as well. Perhaps one lesson, and this time reaching beyond these countries, is that while it takes a long time and much persistence to build a democracy (see: Iraq and Afghanistan), it may take much work to destroy one as well.

Establishment Fatigue

For Erdogan's personal brand, meanwhile, another challenge appears to be "establishment fatigue" given his decades-long hold on power. There was a time when Recep Tayyip Erdogan—whether you liked him or not—represented change. He stood for a forward-looking vision for the country, along with the suggestion that he could navigate the most pressing challenges, from the Kurdish issue to corruption to economic mismanagement, and he showed he could do so. The people loved him for this reason and supported him at the ballot box. Now, however, Erdogan's reputation for competence has dwindled.

There was also a time when Erdogan could blame Turkey's Kemalists for treating the country's pious citizens, who sought to overtly display their religious devotion, as second-class citizens. In 2013, Erdogan's comment "that Turkey's existing alcohol laws had been made by 'two drunkards' was taken by many as a reference to Ataturk, part of a polarizing rhetoric that contributed to a summer of violent protest a few weeks later."[14] Now, not even the most ardent Erdogan supporter would deny that the second-class tag goes to the secular crowd. In short, Erdogan's victimization narrative has evidently grown stale and outdated, and younger conservatives do not view him as energizing in the same way that their parents and grandparents did.

For a long time, finally, Erdogan could blame the country's former elites for Turkey's various problems, but he cannot convincingly do this anymore. The economy, Erdogan's responsibility for the past two decades, is a core example. The broad swath of the electorate recognizes that he, and only he, is responsible for its sluggish state.

As of early 2021, Erdogan has decided that his way out of this conundrum is more oppression, coupled with rhetoric casting his opponents as terrorists and elites simultaneously. To this end, he has even portrayed students at a top Turkish university as being linked to terrorist groups. On January 8, 2021, Erdogan called those who oppose him terrorists, while his ally, Nationalist Action Party (MHP) head Devlet Bahceli, called for a legal ban targeting the opposition Peoples' Democratic Party (HDP), labeling its members as terrorism supporters. As these events were unfolding, Erdogan appointed former pro-AKP politician Melih Bulu as rector of Bogazici University, Turkey's premier public higher learning institution, where the brightest high school graduates are enrolled. This appointment, the first in recent memory in which a Bogazici outsider was named to head the university, triggered a reaction from the school's students and faculty alike, as well as broader opposition factions. Pro-Erdogan pundits jumped in to paint naysayers as "elites." It is not certain, though, that Erdogan's strategy of casting his opponents as terrorists and elites will work, especially with the rising younger generation.

Demographic Trends

The current national divide is puzzling to Erdogan's opponents, including most significantly Turkish millennials, who have come of age under him, and who lack a strong memory of the twentieth-century Turkish model against which the president has framed his own leadership. They may also lack a personal familiarity with Turkey's "tribalism," wherein key blocs (secularists, then Erdoganists) demand rights for themselves while seeking to deny rights to others.[15]

Thus, since 2003, Erdogan has flooded Turkey's traditionally secularist government and educational institutions with his conservative brand of religion, seeking to raise a "pious generation" in his own image. In primary-school religion classes, for instance, students are taught to embrace jihad as the love of homeland.[16] Jihad, in this Turkish interpretation, involves political Islamism rather than violent uprising.

Moreover, whereas Turkey once had a General Directorate for Women's Affairs, since July 2018 it has been merged into a Ministry of Family, Labor, and Social Services, reflecting a preference for promoting traditional values over equality and empowerment. Erdogan has further granted the government media watchdog sweeping oversight of radio and television broadcasting, to filter out content at odds with its conservative worldview. On-screen, even kissing is considered obscene, and depictions of alcohol and tobacco consumption are blurred. Meanwhile, a heavy dose of violence and glorification of violence specifically against women is tolerated.

But Erdogan's top-down social conservativism appears to be a losing proposition with the millennials.[17] Surveys show an overwhelming commitment to liberal democratic values among this group, which constitutes as much as a third of the electorate—a first for *any* demographic cohort in Turkey.[18] Its members are also far less religious than previous generations, and twice as likely to be deist or atheist relative to the national average. Only a quarter pray regularly, in contrast to the nearly half of the population that does.[19] Voters between the ages of eighteen and twenty-nine comprised 25 percent of the electorate in the most recent general election, and will comprise an even larger share in 2023.[20]

Support for the Turkish president is also dropping among young voters who self-identify as conservative. Max Hoffman, writing for the Center for American Progress about Erdogan's shrinking influence, explains that "the AKP's biggest accomplishments in conservative minds—such as the lifting of the headscarf ban or the improvement of healthcare and municipal services—are taken for granted by many of those who came of age in the past decade."[21]

What is more, young conservatives appear to be embracing less rigid ideologies than their parents.[22] They are increasingly forming their views based on social media news sources, which foster greater openness to opposition voices, as opposed to narrowly focused government television outlets. All in all, conservative, younger citizens tend now to more often perceive Erdogan as "the best out of bad options."[23]

In a survey about women's head coverings, just 47 percent of women between the ages of eighteen and thirty-two were found to use them, compared to 62 percent of all women in the country, indicating a broader disavowal of public piety.[24] This majority foreswearing the headscarf—a first for any demographic since the formation of the Turkish republic—suggests the realization, under the political Islamist Erdogan, of at least one component of Ataturk's secularist dream.

According to Turkish pollster Bekir Agirdir, among 19 million young Turkish citizens between roughly ages eighteen and forty, 2 million are "global citizens," referring to the highly educated who value diversity, reject gender inequality, and seek involvement in "horizontal structures," such as crosscutting social and online groups, to achieve results for society.[25] Such movements are quickly growing in popularity nationally, fostering a youth generation with a radically different understanding of civic participation than their predecessors—perhaps a good sign for Turkey's democratic future.[26] In 2020, massive protests arose across Turkey due to the homicide of Pinar Gultekin, a twenty-seven-year-old woman brutally murdered by her boyfriend. Femicide remains a prevalent human rights issue in Turkey, and protests led by youth activists prevented the country from withdrawing from an international convention on the topic.[27]

Such civil society efforts offer hope for Turkey's future. Since the early nineteenth century, when the Ottoman sultans launched a Westernization drive, state and state-connected elites have led Turkey's modernization efforts. Now, however, civil society seems to be taking on this task, with the state falling behind. The future of Turkey is in the hands of its citizens, and not the state or those connected to it— for the first time in modern history.

Notes

1   Soner Cagaptay and Deniz Yuksel, "Turkey's COVID-19 Response," *Caravan*, Hoover Institution, June 4, 2020, available at https://www. washingtoninstitute.org/policy-analysis/turkeys-covid-19-response; Tessa Fox, "In Turkey Erdogan Is Playing Politics with Coronavirus Relief," *Foreign Policy*, April 17, 2020, https://foreignpolicy. com/2020/04/17/erdogan-turkey-coronavirus-relief-politics-akp-chp-brother-tayyip-soup-kitchen/.

2   Daren Butler, "Turkey's Fight Against Coronavirus Fails to Heal Divisions, Opponents Say," Reuters, April 9, 2020, https://uk.reuters. com/article/us-health-coronavirus-turkey-campaign/turkeys-fight-against-coronavirus-fails-to-heal-divisions-opponents-say-idUKKCN21R2C9.

3   "Has Turkey Lost Control of the Coronavirus Pandemic?" Deutsche Welle, December 15, 2020, https://www.dw.com/en/has-turkey-lost-control-of-the-coronavirus-pandemic/a-55952967.

4   For a detailed treatment of Turkey's new presidential system, see Selim Koru, "The Institutional Structure of 'New Turkey,'" Foreign Policy Research Institute, February 2021, https://www.fpri.org/article/2021/02/the-institutional-structure-of-new-turkey/.

5   Dennis Ross, "Coalition Maintenance in the Soviet Union," *World Politics* 32, no. 2 (January 1980): 258–80.

6   "Outcry as Turkey Orders Rerun of Istanbul Mayoral Election," *Guardian*, May 6, 2019, https://www.theguardian.com/world/2019/may/06/turkey-orders-rerun-of-istanbul-election-in-blow-to-opposition.

7   Carlotta Gall, "Turkey's President Suffers Stinging Defeat in Istanbul Election Redo," *New York Times*, June 23, 2019, https://www.nytimes. com/2019/06/23/world/europe/istanbul-mayor-election-erdogan. html; "Erdogan's Party Suffers Blow After Istanbul Re-Run Poll Defeat," BBC News, June 24, 2019, https://www.bbc.com/news/world-europe-48739256.

8 "Finance Minister Berat Albayrak Announces Resignation on Instagram," *Duvar English*, November 8, 2020, https://www.duvarenglish.com/economy/2020/11/08/finance-minister-berat-albayrak-announces-resignation-on-instagram.

9 Murat Yetkin, "Why and How Turkish Finance Minister Resigned," Yetkin Report, November 9, 2020, https://yetkinreport.com/en/2020/11/09/why-and-how-turkish-finance-minister-resigned/.

10 "Treasury and Finance Minister Berat Albayrak Resigns from His Post," *Daily Sabah*, November 9, 2020, https://www.dailysabah.com/politics/treasury-and-finance-minister-berat-albayrak-resigns-from-his-post/news; Associated Press, "Erdogan Accepts Turkish Finance Minister's Resignation," November 9, 2020, https://apnews.com/article/turkey-recep-tayyip-erdogan-financial-markets-europe-economy-1468ad546ebdac6da4daf757bb088cf1.

11 Soner Cagaptay, "Erdogan's Presidential System Isn't Working. The Istanbul Election Shows Why," *Washington Post*, June 24, 2019, https://www.washingtonpost.com/opinions/2019/06/25/erdogans-presidential-system-isnt-working-istanbul-election-shows-why/.

12 Nick Ashdown, "A Motorcycle-Riding Leftist Feminist Is Coming for Erdogan," *Foreign Policy*, May 1, 2020, https://foreignpolicy.com/2020/05/01/canan-kaftancioglu-turkey-erdogan-chp-profile/.

13 Nora Fisher Onar, "Are 'Global Cities' an Antidote to Populism and Nationalism? Istanbul Offers Some Hope," *Washington Post*, July 19, 2018, https://www.washingtonpost.com/news/monkey-cage/wp/2018/07/19/are-global-cities-an-antidote-to-populism-and-nationalism-istanbul-offers-some-hope/.

14 Reuters, "Turkey's Kemalists See Secularist Legacy Under Threat," November 17, 2013, https://www.reuters.com/article/us-turkey-kemalists/turkeys-kemalists-see-secularist-legacy-under-threat-idUSBRE9AG0HQ20131118.

15 I would like to thank Deniz Yuksel for helping draft this section of the book.

16 Dan Bilefsky, "In Turkey's New Curriculum, Ataturk, Darwin and Jihad Get Face-Lifts," *New York Times*, September 18, 2017, https://www.nytimes.com/2017/09/18/world/europe/turkey-curriculum-darwin-jihad.html.

17 Max Hoffman, "Turkey's President Erdogan Is Losing Ground at Home," Center for American Progress, August 24, 2020, https://www.americanprogress.org/issues/security/reports/2020/08/24/489727/turkeys-president-erdogan-losing-ground-home/.

18 "How Different Are Youth from Society, 2018," Konda Interactif, https://interaktif.konda.com.tr/en/Youth2018/#secondPage.

19 Ibid.

20 Hoffman, "Turkey's President Erdogan Is Losing Ground," https://www.americanprogress.org/issues/security/reports/2020/08/24/489727/turkeys-president-erdogan-losing-ground-home/.

21 Ibid.

22 Ibid.

23 Ibid.

24 "5 Temel Degiskenden Olusan 104 Kumenin Toplum Icindeki Oranlari," Konda Interaktif, https://interaktif.konda.com.tr/tr/tr2018_matris/.

25 "KONDA Genel Muduru Agirdir: AKP'nin 'Dindar Nesil' Muhendisligi Tutmadi; Oruc Tutan, Namaz Kilanlarin Orani Dustu," T24, December 11, 2019, https://t24.com.tr/video/konda-genel-muduru-agirdir-akp-nin-dindar-nesil-muhendisligi-tutmadi-oruc-tutan-namaz-kilanlarin-orani-dustu,24966.

26 Orhan Kemal Cengiz, "Environmental Problems Provoke Protests on All Fronts in Turkey," Al-Monitor, August 12, 2019, https://www.al-monitor.com/pulse/originals/2019/08/turkey-environmental-problems-provoke-protests.html.

27 "Turkey Mulls Withdrawing from Violence Against Women Treaty," Al-Monitor, August 5, 2020, https://www.al-monitor.com/pulse/originals/2020/08/turkey-istanbul-convention-femicide-women-violence.html.

9

Erdogan's Game Plan

None of the trends discussed here means that Erdogan will go down without a fight or that he will go down at all. Nor do the various challenges to his political survival necessarily suggest a bright future for democracy in Turkey. Namely, with the economic impact of the pandemic further eroding his popularity, a period of intensified authoritarianism will ensue in Turkey, driven by Erdogan's instinct for political survival.

Being voted out could well be Erdogan's deepest fear, given the many enemies he has made. Trouble looms should he exit the presidency. Typically, when Turkish presidents leave office, they retire to a villa in Istanbul, or along the Turkish Riviera, and some even take up hobbies such as painting. Erdogan must sense his prospects would be grimmer, considering how many of his opponents he has brutalized, starting with the case of the Ergenekon trials of 2008–11. He likely would fear a post-presidency darkened by prosecution, or even persecution.

However, Erdogan knows he need not win the next elections with 60–70 percent support. Hence, his manifold strategy: first, as explained earlier, deliver economic growth once again—including by launching a charm offensive aimed at the United States and encouraging foreign direct investment flows into the country—in order to rebuild his base. Then, in a slightly more Machiavellian way this time, launch a "full-court press" reelection strategy, simultaneously oppressing, overwhelming, dividing, and distracting his opponents to peel away 1 percent from the opposition here, 1 percent there. All this ties into Erdogan's overall electoral goal: reach 50 percent plus 1.

Embracing "Reform" While Inventing New Enemies

As Erdogan surveys the political landscape, he undoubtedly sees two fundamental options: either embrace democracy and watch an increasingly unfriendly electorate vote him out, or become more authoritarian still, in an attempt to fend off the country's demographic, economic, and political trends. But Erdogan is a Janus-faced politician, which means he can do both, at least tactically speaking. To this end, the "democratic reform package" he will likely unveil in 2021 could include the jail release of some civil society activists, to allay fears in the Biden White House and across European capitals over Turkey's democratic backslide. But simultaneously, he will maintain his nativist populist tactics at home. This latter reality, of course, will be deeply unfortunate—and tragic—for marginalized groups such as women, liberals, secularists, leftists, Christians, and the LGBT community.

In pursuing this path, Erdogan will also be compelled to invent new enemies—domestic and foreign—and new conspiracies similar to the 2008 Ergenekon plot, all to justify further persecuting his opponents and their leaders, starting with the HDP. Erdogan has already jailed Selahattin Demirtas, the leader of the pro–Kurdish nationalist and progressive alliance, and he might even target the leadership of main-opposition CHP and others. Overall, though, for reasons I explain below, the HDP will bear the brunt of Erdogan's demonization strategy.

Boosting Splinter Opposition Parties

To date, Erdogan's greatest political achievement, arguably, has been the 2018 move to an executive-style presidency, which resulted in his effective crowning as the first quasi-sultan of Turkey's second republic. But this switch has also, inadvertently, created Erdogan's greatest electoral challenge: a unified opposition.

For a long time, Erdogan was blessed with a disparate opposition, with various strands representing Turkish and Kurdish nationalists, secularists, and conservatives, among others. The gap between those opposition factions was often wider than the gap separating them from Erdogan. This, together with the economic growth the Turkish leader delivered until lately, helped him win many successive elections. But the presidential system requires a two-way race, with the winner needing to take more than half the vote, a reality that has forced the opposition to unite. The first such alliance fell short in the 2018 presidential race, but in 2019 opposition mayoral candidate Ekrem Imamoglu won Istanbul using the same approach, with the full spectrum of Turkey's opposition rallying behind him.

Now, Erdogan wants to divide the opposition by boosting splinter opposition parties that appeal to the base of his main opponent, the CHP. Examples include the recently established Movement for Change in Turkey, led by former CHP politician Mustafa Sarigul, and another new party, launched in early 2021 by CHP figure Muharrem Ince. These blocs have miraculously received much airtime on Erdogan-backed networks, while other factions, such as those led by Davutoglu and Babacan, are spurned.[1] Whether these parties can capture more than a few percentage points of support is uncertain, but even that could be enough to keep Erdogan in office.

...While Ignoring Violence Against the Real Opposition

Along these lines, violence against opposition politicians, including a January 15, 2021, mob attack in broad daylight on Future Party vice chair Selcuk Ozdag outside his Ankara home, also deserves attention.[2] Coupled with other anti-opposition attacks—including a lynch mob attempt against main opposition CHP chair Kemal Kilicdaroglu during the 2019 local elections and frequent attacks against HDP offices[3]—a wave of nonlethal "low-level" violence against opposition politicians, opinion makers, and journalists could intimidate the opposition just enough to eke out a victory for Erdogan in the next elections. Erdogan does not seek landslide support, but rather just a simple majority, and such tactics serve as stepping-stones to this goal.

Choosing Between Two Kurdish Nationalist Factions: MHP and IYI

This all means that Erdogan's own party, the AKP, need not be dominant or his only vehicle to win. In 2001, at its inception, the party included diverse voices and political forces, constituting a heterogeneous bloc of rightist and centrist actors. Still, at its center were Erdogan and other politicians from the Turkish National Outlook school of political Islam, such as the Welfare Party (Refah). During Erdogan's first years as prime minister, mirroring his own rise in popularity, support for the AKP increased from 36 percent in 2002 to nearly 50 percent in 2011, leaving him comfortable enough to dispense with most non-political-Islamist allies, including business liberals and center-right politicians. Subsequently, by the early 2010s, political Islamists became undeniably dominant within the AKP. In recent years, Erdogan went so far as to cut ties with even key National Outlook figures such as Abdullah Gul, a fellow AKP member who formerly served as the country's president.

The AKP is now, sadly, a shell of its old self, peopled by Erdogan loyalists who have joined the president and his party only in recent years, including many in Erdogan's cabinet. When he needs electoral support, the president can turn further to the right-wing MHP and also help build other factions that might benefit from an alliance with his party. Such a move, notably, would prompt an even harder line by Erdogan on the Kurdish issue both domestically, against the PKK, and in Syria, against the group's YPG offshoot, with the goal of currying favor with MHP leader Devlet Bahceli and his base.

Yet Erdogan's dalliance with the MHP carries its own risks, given that Bahceli's hardline nationalism cost the AKP in the Istanbul mayoral vote and that Istanbul is home to millions of Kurdish-speaking voters. Therefore, the Turkish president could opt to turn instead to the more moderately Turkish nationalist Good Party (IYI) and its leader, Meral Aksener. Such a move, allowing the president to adopt a less strident Turkish nationalist attitude domestically, thereby winning back some Kurdish voters in Istanbul and elsewhere who have abandoned him, could help Erdogan's bloc clinch victory at the ballot box.

But this path too will be complicated. When Aksener herself broke away from the MHP in October 2017 to form the IYI, the split roughly followed pro- and anti-Erdogan lines inside the MHP. It is therefore unlikely that a majority of IYI supporters, who despise Erdogan as much as they like Aksener, would follow her should she enter an electoral alliance with the president.

Demonizing the HDP to Get IYI on Board

In the short term, this scenario leaves Erdogan with the hardline MHP as his key electoral ally, unless of course he can somehow convince Aksener's base that the IYI is allied with "terrorists," prompting Aksener to quit the opposition bloc. To this end, Erdogan will demonize Kurdish nationalists to force the IYI to abandon the opposition bloc. Accordingly, Erdogan has recently lashed out at HDP leaders, tagging the jailed party head, Selahattin Demirtas, as a "terrorist" who "has the blood of thousands of Kurds on his hands."[4]

Turkish politics has historically been right-wing dominated. Parties on the right have led national governments in all but seventeen months since 1950, excluding four years spent under military rule, following the coups of 1960, 1973, and 1980. Aksener's faction is the only significant member of the opposition bloc challenging Erdogan. If she leaves the opposition, Erdogan wins.

Finding New Wars

Erdogan wants to play it safe and simultaneously strengthen his base by engaging in new foreign policy ventures, reminding voters of his strongman image globally, as he did in late 2020 when Ankara boosted support to its ally Azerbaijan against Armenia in the South Caucasus. He will also launch new campaigns against the PKK and its affiliates in Iraq and Syria, moves that will receive significant support on both sides of the political aisle. Not even the possibility of a dogfight with Greece or a skirmish with Turkey's smaller neighbors such as Cyprus—driven by Turkish natural gas drilling activity off the Cypriot coast, or a fresh Turkish incursion into Syria targeting the YPG—should be ruled out. These could all be means to solidify his right-wing base and divert attention from troubles at home. The combination of such engagements with Turkey's real foreign policy concerns, stretching all across the region, could likewise help the Turkish president broaden his national security constituency.

Exerting Even More Pressure on Opposition Factions

At the same time, and in order to contain democratic opposition within Turkey, Erdogan will further limit freedoms of assembly, association, media, and expression. To this end, the AKP-led Turkish parliament passed a sweeping social media bill on July 29, 2020, giving Erdogan unbridled power to control social media content across a wide variety of platforms. This law requires platforms such as Twitter and Facebook to appoint Turkey-based representatives to be subservient to government authorities and meet deadlines for removal of content deemed inappropriate by the state.[5] For a country with 13 million Twitter users, and given that the vast majority of domestic media outlets are under the state's hand, this is not only a repudiation of freedom of expression, but a means of further limiting Turkish citizens' access to basic information—a right already stretched thin.

The social media legislation is a grave omen with possibly monumental consequences. Even before the law's enactment, Turkey issued more Twitter content-removal requests than any other country, so the law's passage intimates a dire clampdown on free expression.[6] Erdogan knows this bill can affect his entire opposition, not just a segment or two. In a blatant recent move against a new rival, Erdogan in summer 2020 ordered the closure of Istanbul Sehir University, which was established by ally-turned-opponent Ahmet Davutoglu, founder in late December 2019 of the Gelecek (Future) Party. Davutoglu has embraced freedom of speech as a core ideological tenet and blamed Erdogan for its demise under his leadership.

...And Moving Goalposts Farther for the Opposition

Similarly, Erdogan will likely use his control of the legislature to enact a new electoral law, moving the goalpost yet farther for the opposition. Turkey has one of the highest electoral thresholds of any democracy, requiring parties to garner 10 percent of the popular vote to enter parliament. In the last parliamentary elections, in 2018, however, smaller opposition parties that formed electoral coalitions with the CHP (IYI formally; Saadet and HDP informally and on a constituency-by-constituency basis) were able to bypass this requirement thanks to their combined vote percentage. What is more, this opposition alliance famously denied Erdogan's candidates a victory in the 2019 mayoral elections.

Realizing this, Erdogan is seeking to implement stricter measures to stop additional smaller parties from boosting the opposition bloc. New legislation could require parties in electoral alliances to pass a threshold of 5–7 percent individually to be represented in parliament.[7] It is unlikely that smaller parties, such as Saadet (SP, also known as Felicity), former foreign minister and prime minister Ahmet Davutoglu's Gelecek (Future), the Democracy and Progress Party (DEVA), led by former AKP finance minister Ali Babacan, or perhaps even the HDP, would pass this threshold as single entities.

While negotiations between Erdogan and his ally MHP leader Bahceli continue as of early 2021, it is certain that whatever legislation Erdogan passes through the country's parliament to this end will benefit his AKP and the MHP, barring smaller opposition factions from the legislature and undermining the overall strength of the anti-Erdogan bloc. In fact, Bahceli may be the clincher of this legislative deal, given that his faction's support to the AKP provides the Turkish president's party with a majority in parliament. This means any legislation Bahceli consents to regarding the new electoral law or other changes will have to be so fine-tuned, gerrymandered, and hocus-pocus that it would—simultaneously—cripple his nemeses IYI and HDP at the ballot box, blocking their path to parliament, while avoiding a similar effect on Bahceli's own small faction.

Notes

1 See Soner Cagaptay (@SonerCagaptay), "New trend in Turkish politics: faux opposition parties (backed by pro-Erdogan media). While such factions may not garner more than few percent points support, they fit into Erdogan's overall electoral strategy: Peel 1 % from the opposition here and 1 % there—to get to 50 % + 1," post on Twitter, February 8, 2021, 11:02 a.m., https://twitter.com/SonerCagaptay/status/1358808352839581696.

2 "Dissident Politician and Journalist Severely Beaten in Ankara," *Arab News*, January 15, 2021, https://www.arabnews.com/node/1793276/middle-east.

3 "Turkey: Is Mob Violence Undermining Democracy?" Deutsche Welle, May 3, 2019, https://www.dw.com/en/turkey-is-mob-violence-undermining-democracy/a-48598883; "Pro-Kurdish Party's Istanbul Office Targeted in Armed Attack," Duvar English, January 15, 2020, https://www.duvarenglish.com/politics/2020/01/15/pro-kurdish-partys-istanbul-office-targeted-in-armed-attack.

4 Ece Toksabay and Daren Butler, "Erdogan Slams Jailed Kurdish Leader, Fuelling Scepticism About Reform Pledge," Reuters, November 25, 2020, https://www.reuters.com/article/uk-turkey-politics-demirtas-idUKKBN28518F.

5 "Turkey's New Social Media Law Put into Effect," *Hurriyet Daily News*, July 31, 2020, https://www.hurriyetdailynews.com/turkeys-new-social-media-law-put-into-effect-157029.

6 "Turkey's President Cracks Down on Social Media," *Economist*, August 8, 2020, https://www.economist.com/europe/2020/08/06/turkeys-president-cracks-down-on-social-media.

7 "Abdulkadir Selvi: Ittifak Halinde Giren Partiler icin Secim Barajinin Yuzde 12 Olmasi Secenegi," *Diken*, January 7, 2021, http://www.diken.com.tr/abdulkadir-selvi-ittifak-halinde-giren-partiler-icin-secim-barajinin-yuzde-12-olmasi-secenegi/.

10

But Will He Succeed?

Ironically for Erdogan, although the 2018 switch to a presidential system has made him Turkey's most powerful president since the country became a multiparty democracy in 1950, it has also strengthened his opposition. For years, Erdogan was blessed with an ineffective opposition composed of disparate groups—leftists and rightists, Kurdish and Turkish nationalists—who could not countenance voting for each other's candidate. Indeed, under the parliamentary system, a party could form a government with as little as 40 percent of the vote—and sometimes less, as in the AKP's 34 percent triumph in 2002. Now, however, the presidential system requires a runoff if no single candidate clears 50 percent. Realizing that it would have no chance without unity, the opposition offered up joint candidate Muharrem Ince, of the CHP, in the 2018 presidential elections. Ince lost decisively, but the joint approach bore fruit in the next year's municipal vote in Istanbul.

Can the Opposition Stay Together?

At this stage, the opposition can block Erdogan only if its four key parties—the secularist and leftist CHP, the political Islamist and religious-conservative Saadet, the Turkish nationalist and center-right IYI, and, informally, the Kurdish nationalist and progressive HDP—stay together, while also bringing along Davutoglu's recently established center-right and conservative Gelecek (Future) and Babacan's centrist and business liberal DEVA. Broadening and then sustaining such a "rainbow coalition" is indeed a tall order, not just in Turkey, where the opposition will face a crackdown by Erdogan, but in just about any country facing a similar situation. Consequently, as noted before, Erdogan's key moves will be aimed at undermining the opposition bloc, especially by highlighting differences between the IYI and HDP.

By Embracing Radical Love

Another challenge for the opposition factions will be to avoid getting lured into the president's style of politics. Erdogan's opponents have long tried attacking his nativist populist constituents as a means of defeating him at the ballot box. Specifically, oppositionists have targeted Erdogan's base as "religious fanatics," while even sometimes suggesting these voters pick him because he bribes them with gifts.[1] And when Erdogan has criticized opposition leaders, such as CHP chair Kilicdaroglu, the latter have tried in vain to compete against Erdogan on his own turf: nativist populist demagoguery.

But in the 2019 Istanbul mayoral vote, Ekrem Imamoglu embraced a unique communications strategy against the AKP candidate, dubbed "radical love." The campaign's effectiveness suggests that the only way to defeat a populist leader might be by embracing or "loving" the populist base.[2] Imamoglu's campaign manager said shortly after the victory, "We had two simple rules: Ignore Erdogan and love those who love Erdogan."[3]

Accordingly, Imamoglu avoided getting into a political mud-wrestling match with Erdogan even when provoked; for example, on the campaign trail, Erdogan had accused his party of working with terrorists—implying the PKK—because of its Kurdish outreach.[4] What is more, Imamoglu made an effort to reach out to conservative voters, spending significant time campaigning in their neighborhoods rather than those populated by liberal and secular voters. A united opposition embracing "radical love" would therefore appear to stand a chance of defeating Erdogan at the ballot box, though Erdogan will do everything he can to pull the opposition into direct confrontation with him, such as by launching new culture wars over gender issues and other topics that the opposition will find difficult to ignore.

And Using Its Good Governance Advantage

Erdogan's poor handling of the pandemic has highlighted the effectiveness of his opponents, while also revealing disputes within his *saray* (palace advisors).[5] Specifically, the earlier-noted pandemic-remediation initiatives by the mayors of Istanbul and Ankara have allowed these figures to emerge as problem solvers. Erdogan, long the face of progress and effective governance, has resembled a laggard during the Covid era. Moreover, these opposition mayors, especially Imamoglu and Yavas, while lacking access to mainstream platforms, have used social media to roll out near-daily initiatives to fight the pandemic. They have thus also secured control of the narrative.

To the extent that the Turkish opposition does not fracture—and that its leaders continue to govern effectively and apply their "radical love" strategy—it stands a chance of defeating Erdogan at the ballot box. Whether Erdogan will accept any such defeat is less certain.

How Will Europe and the United States
Respond to Erdogan?

Ultimately, Erdogan will avoid any serious concessions to his opposition that could threaten his electoral prospects. In other words, he will make it look as if he is ending his crackdown at home, while still actually clenching the reins of power.

In this regard, Europe and the United States have a role to play, at least as far as Erdogan is concerned. If he calls snap elections to take advantage of Turkey's possible economic recovery following the Covid pandemic, he will hope for the United States and Europe to target him rhetorically beforehand, allowing him to turn the contest into a matter of national pride and sovereignty. This would comport with his successful strategy in recent years, when he has cast himself as Turkey's (and, by extension, Islam's) only true defender against such attacks from the West—including Turkey's European and NATO allies, which have often criticized Erdogan for his antidemocratic and other transgressions. For these allies, public diplomacy strategy will have to be fine-tuned so that criticizing Erdogan's administration is acceptable, but attacking or trolling Turkey or its citizens is not.

By indeed showing a willingness to adopt this approach, just as Erdogan's opposition has embraced radical love and avoided culture wars with the president, many of Turkey's European and NATO allies have now eschewed messaging that could be seen as attacking Turkey and its citizens. When Erdogan reconverted Hagia Sophia into a mosque in July 2020, European countries and Washington were mostly quiet, denying Erdogan a popularity-boosting instrument. Notably, only Greece—which has special religious, political, and historic ties to this former Byzantine cathedral—and France attacked Erdogan *and* Turkey.

Potential Tensions with France

The Great Power dynamics discussed earlier could lead to a generally fractious era between Paris and Ankara. And Erdogan, for his part, has much fodder for lambasting the French, including Paris's opposition to Ankara's position in Libya and the eastern Mediterranean, where France backs Greece. What is more, French support to the PKK offshoot YPG in Syria could greatly unnerve many of Turkey's citizens, including Erdogan's opponents such as those in the IYI camp, should Erdogan promote the issue. At the same time, Paris increasingly views Ankara through the prism of civilizational and identity politics.[6]

For its own part, France, unlike its EU neighbor Germany, has embraced a policy of blaming and shaming Erdogan for his democratic transgressions and foreign policy endeavors, and accordingly French president Emmanuel Macron often targets Erdogan in personal terms. In June 2020, Macron did not hold back from accusing the Turkish president of "playing a dangerous game" in the eastern Mediterranean and Libya, and Macron has continued to pronounce that Turkey has no chance of joining the EU.[7] In the same month, Paris claimed the Turkish navy "illuminated" a French vessel with radar.[8] Macron's reelection campaign for France's 2022 presidential vote, meanwhile, coincides with the prospect of Turkish snap elections. All this suggests potentially rocky future ties and a potential NATO hotspot centered on Ankara-Paris.[9]

Biden's Act

Erdogan, a student of American presidents for nearly two decades, knows how to transform himself into the figure they want as a Turkish counterpart. For Bush, a faithful Christian, Erdogan was the "faithful Muslim" in return; for Obama, who wished to communicate with

Muslims, Erdogan was a "window to the Muslim world"; and for the deal-loving Trump, Erdogan was a dealmaker. Accordingly, Erdogan will undoubtedly seek to become whatever Biden wishes him to be—at least in the short term.

But Biden too is a student of his fellow politicians, including Erdogan. When he served as Obama's vice president, he met Erdogan numerous times. What is more, once Erdogan-Obama ties cooled after 2013 owing to differences over the Egyptian uprising and the fall of Mohamed Morsi's government—Erdogan called it a coup and blamed Obama for the Islamist leader's fall[10]—Biden became Obama's interlocutor with the Turkish leader.

Biden's familiarity with Erdogan therefore gives him an edge in navigating relations between the two, as well as in sorting through different opinions within his own administration. On the one hand, realpolitik thinkers on the Biden team will argue that the U.S. president must account for Turkey's proximity to Iran and (across the Black Sea) Russia. Turkey policy, in their view, should be crafted in view of U.S. relations with both Iran and Russia. In a worst case scenario, these thinkers will argue, Biden must ensure Ankara is not a spoiler for U.S. policies toward Moscow and Tehran. Others, however, will argue that it is time to push back against Erdogan's democratic transgressions and budding ties with Putin and that a new approach to Turkey is needed in Washington.

In any case, getting Erdogan fully onboard with U.S. policies regarding Russia could be a tall order given the overall minefield Biden must immediately navigate with the Turkish president. One such issue involves the PKK/YPG. The Turkish incursion into northeast Syria in 2019 pushed the YPG away from the Turkish border, making the group less of an imminent danger to Ankara. At the same time, Turkish drone and military campaigns against PKK leadership and bases in Iraq have inflicted damage,[11] while a successful counterterrorism campaign inside Turkey has crippled much of the organization's domestic infrastructure.[12] This leaves an opening for Ankara and Washington to find a midway solution to the PKK-YPG issue—for instance, with Turkey acquiescing to continued U.S.-YPG cooperation against the Islamic State in return for PKK cadres leaving Turkey and also moving farther away from the Turkish-Syrian border.

An even trickier issue will be potential U.S.-court-imposed sanctions against Turkish-government-owned Halkbank for violating U.S. sanctions targeting Iran.[13] If any sanctions are rolled out against a major Turkish bank in 2021, with Turkey's finances being in such bad shape, this will almost certainly weaken the national economic outlook further, quashing Erdogan's hopes for a strong postpandemic rally and subsequent victory in potential snap elections.

Finally, of course, will be Biden's challenge of managing the S-400 issue. It is unlikely, as noted, that Erdogan will return the missile-defense system to Putin. The Russian president wants to use the missile-defense issue to permanently cleave Ankara from Washington, and Erdogan currently sees Putin as his protector—and thus will be highly disinclined to offend him.

Biden would basically have to accept Putin's machinations, commit completely to militarily backing Turkey's positions in Syria, Libya, and South Caucasus, and look the other way regarding Erdogan's democratic transgressions to achieve full harmony with his Turkish counterpart. This certainly will not happen, and given Erdogan's preference for his own survival over that of Turkish democracy, Biden will almost inevitably find he must distance himself from Erdogan.

Notes

1 "AKP ne Kadar Bedava Komur Dagitti," *Hurriyet*, November 5, 2008, https://www.hurriyet.com.tr/gundem/akp-ne-kadar-bedava-komur-dagitti-10289233.

2 Melvyn Ingleby, "A Turkish Opposition Leader Is Fighting Erdogan with 'Radical Love,'" *Atlantic*, June 14, 2019, https://www.theatlantic.com/international/archive/2019/06/ex-istanbul-mayor-imamoglu-fights-erdogan-radical-love/591541/.

3 Carlotta Gall, "How a Message of Unity and Mistakes by Erdogan Tipped the Istanbul Election," *New York Times*, June 26, 2019, https://www.nytimes.com/2019/06/26/world/europe/istanbul-mayor-imamoglu-erdogan.html.

4 Ayla Jean Yackley, "The Triumphant New Face of Turkey's Resurgent Political Opposition," *The New Yorker*, June 30, 2020, https://www.newyorker.com/news/dispatch/the-triumphant-new-face-of-turkeys-resurgent-political-opposition.

5 Soner Cagaptay and Deniz Yuksel, "Turkey's COVID-19 Response," *Caravan*, Hoover Institution, June 4, 2020, https://www.hoover.org/research/turkeys-covid-19-response.

6 Selim Koru, email exchange with author, February 28, 2021.

7 Michael Daventry, "Emmanuel Macron: 'Turkey Is Playing a Dangerous Game in Libya,'" Euronews, June 23, 2020, https://www.euronews.com/2020/06/23/emmanuel-macron-turkey-is-playing-a-dangerous-game-in-libya.

8 See, e.g., Associated Press, "Turkey Insists on Apology from France over Naval Standoff," Bloomberg, July 17, 2020, https://www.bloomberg.com/news/articles/2020-07-17/turkey-insists-on-apology-from-france-over-naval-standoff.

9 "Turkish Navy Ships Menace French Frigate in the Mediterranean," *Arabia Policy*, June 23, 2020, https://arabiapolicy.com/turkish-navy-ships-menace-french-frigate-in-the-mediterranean/.

10 Steven A. Cook, "Egypt and Turkey: Nightmares," Council on Foreign
Relations, November 25, 2013, https://www.cfr.org/blog/egypt-and-
turkey-nightmares.

11 "Conflict Between Turkey and Armed Kurdish Groups," Council on
Foreign Relations, January 27, 2021, https://www.cfr.org/global-conflict-
tracker/conflict/conflict-between-turkey-and-armed-kurdish-groups.

12 Max Hoffman, "The State of the Turkish-Kurdish Conflict," Center for
American Progress, August 12, 2019, https://www.americanprogress.
org/issues/security/reports/2019/08/12/473508/state-turkish-kurdish-
conflict/.

13 "Turkey's Halkbank Urges U.S. Judge to Dismiss Iran Sanctions
Case," Al Jazeera, September 18, 2020, https://www.aljazeera.com/
economy/2020/9/18/turkeys-halkbank-urges-us-judge-to-dismiss-iran-
sanctions-case.

11

The Sultan's Legacy

The Romans measured time by *saecula*—periods of years that pass between the occurrence of an incident and the death of all the people alive at the time of the incident. Ataturk's republic is not yet one *saeculum* old, and the memory of Ottoman greatness still resonates deeply with Turkey's citizens. Ataturk, who ruled Turkey between 1923 and 1938, shaped the republic in his own image. Erdogan has now, as of 2021, exceeded Ataturk's tenure, having governed for eighteen years. In that time, he has successfully torn down, or recalibrated, much of Ataturk's legacy. But under Erdogan, the country has also reverted to an authoritarian style of government more reminiscent of the Ataturk years—and those of his successor, Ismet Inonu (r. 1938–50)—than of the late twentieth century.

As the "new Ataturk," Erdogan has recast Turkey's top-down system in his own image: profoundly Islamic and socially conservative. Erdogan's new Turkey primarily faces not Europe or the West, but the Middle East and the "Muslim world." Erdogan wants to see Ankara rising as a great capital, with and through influence over Muslims across Turkey's former Ottoman possessions—especially in the Middle East, but also from the Balkans in the west to competing against Iran in the east, in the fashion of the sixteenth-century Ottoman sultan Selim the Grim.

For good or bad, Erdogan has reminded Turkey's citizens of their imperial legacy, and he has also flooded the country's education system and government with religion. Even if changes are made to the country's educational curricula after he is gone, his legacy will reverberate for some time. Similarly, some element of Turkey's post-Erdogan elites will be prickly on matters of foreign policy, complaining about the country's treatment, creating tensions with competitors near and far, and more often than not reluctant to accept "small country" or "obedient ally" status.

On July 9, 2020, when Turkey's Council of State voided a 1934 Ataturk cabinet decision designating Istanbul's famed Hagia Sophia as a museum, the decision marked a victory for Erdogan in determining the symbolic status of the fifteen-hundred-year-old landmark—one of the world's most extraordinary buildings, jewel of Byzantium, and once the largest interior space in the world. A decade-old constitutional amendment had allowed Erdogan to appoint a majority of the council's current judges, so the decision was not a surprise. But Erdogan's subtler message was something like this: "How dare these secularists deny us pious Muslims the 'liberty' to pray at Hagia Sophia?" As a matter of strategy, Erdogan is seeking to restore his (shrinking) right-wing base by exploiting the controversy to peddle a narrative of victimization.

Such a Hagia Sophia strategy might help Erdogan recover a portion of his previous support, but it likely cannot make up for the erosion caused by the economic swoons since 2018. Only economic growth could restore Erdogan's previous stature. Even so, the campaign likely also has a personal angle, rooted in the "two Erdogans": the politician who clings to power, and the mortal who must relinquish it eventually, at least in death.

Istanbul, where Erdogan was born in 1954, is both a city of mosques and the city of Erdogan's political ascent—where he became nationally known upon becoming mayor in 1994. He benefited from hegemony over Turkey's largest city until he effectively lost it in 2019 to opposition mayor Ekrem Imamoglu. From patronizing large, symbolic mosques in the city of his birth—which already has three "Erdogan" mosques, including one under construction in early 2021—to placing religion at the heart of Turkish society, Erdogan now appears determined to leave his indelible mark on his country.

However, Erdogan's legacy will, of course, be mixed—and more somber than he and his followers would like to believe. Visualize the act—described at the beginning of this book—of forcefully hammering a square peg into a round hole and the shattered chips that would subsequently spray all over the place. One can then imagine the crushed lives, damaged institutions (e.g., Turkey's secular education system), and fractured international friendships (most notably with the United States and Europe) sadly left behind by Erdogan as he attempts to overwhelm the forces that constitute and inform today's Turkey.

Hence, years from now, when Erdogan is gone, Turkey may set up a "truth and reconciliation commission," delivering justice for those individuals and entities demonized and brutalized in the Erdogan era. Some will undoubtedly seek to erase Erdogan's legacy or his memory. If Turkey emerges as a freer, more open society, students will likely be taught that Erdogan's reign undermined Turkish democracy. Schools, roads, and buildings named after the former leader will likely be renamed. Eventually, not much may be left of this leader materially, except for the Camlica "Erdogan" Mosque overlooking Istanbul— next to which he may well be buried, like the Ottoman sultans beside their preferred holy sites.

In addition to the Camlica Mosque, the "Hagia Sophia Mosque" recently consecrated by Erdogan, and the new Taksim Mosque, whose construction is backed by the president—overlooking and reshaping Istanbul's central Taksim Square[1]—complete the trilogy of Erdogan mosques in Turkey's imperial capital and Erdogan's hometown. Many decades down the road, how visitors to the mosques Erdogan has built, and to the ancient Hagia Sophia that he reconsecrated, will remember the Turkish leader depends on his forthcoming policy choices, caught as he is between his ambitions for power and Turkey's resilient ambitions for democracy.

Whatever Erdogan's legacy, worshippers and visitors to the three "Erdogan" mosques in Istanbul will forever remember him as Turkey's most consequential leader in a century, a president in form but a sultan in spirit.

Notes

1 Testifying to the city's Greek heritage, Taksim Square has had a Greek Orthodox Church but no prominent mosque.

Index